Hearts and Times:

The Literature of Memory

Hearts and Times:

The Literature of Memory

Oral Histories
Transcribed and Written

by Ross Talarico

■

KAIROS PRESS

DISTRIBUTED BY ACADEMY CHICAGO PUBLISHERS

Published in 1992
Kairos Press
Thomas R. Leavens, Publisher, Inc.

Distributed by
Academy Chicago Publishers
213 West Institute Place
Chicago, Illinois 60610

Library of Congress Cataloging-in-Publication Data

Talarico, Ross, 1945 –
    Hearts and times : the literature of memory : oral histories /
transcribed and written by Ross Talarico.
       p.   cm.
    ISBN 0-89733-382-9 : $18.00
    1. Aging—Poetry. 2. Oral history—Poetry. I. Title
PS3570.A34H4 1992
811'.54—dc20   92-22948
                                       CIP

Cover design by Judy Olsen, DiDonato Associates, Inc.
Book design by Barbara Spann
Illustrations by Julia Anderson-Miller

Acknowledgments

Grateful acknowledgment to the editors of the following publications, where some of the oral histories first appeared:

Upstate Magazine, July 21, 1987: "Train Ride," "Upstate," "Spring Vows." (Gannett Newspapers)

Upstate Magazine, July 3, 1988: "The Orchard Photograph," "Youth," "The Mansion," "Convertible, 1928." (Gannett Newspapers)

Calling Home: Working Class Women's Writings, ed. Janet Zandy, Rutgers University Press, 1990: "Train Ride," "My Certificate in Negro History," "Hands: A Love Poem."

Rochester Voices: Uncommon Writings from Common People, David Lang Publisher, 1989, NY: "The Proposal," "After Mama's Death," "The Gift," "Giving Up The Cakes," "Last Wave," "Over The Years," "Look Ma, No Hands: A Cop's Memories of an Early Scam."

Gannett Newspapers—*Democrat + Chronicle*, *The Times Union*, Rochester, NY (Op.-Ed. Page): "The Cooling Board," "Silver Dollars, Silver Memories," "The New Shoes."

Contents

Romance

Initiations

Possessions

Seclusions

Foreword

THE REMARKABLE GRANDEUR OF these "histories" of ordinary people rises from the page with all the authority and clarity that one finds in the metaphysical territory of Ross Talarico's own poetry. He has lent his gifted invention to their oral cuttings and has transformed these fragments of memory into a splendid cloth, patterned with the passions and the dreams and the sorrows of our time. Once again to discredit alchemy, these people and their histories reveal themselves to have been pure gold all along.

Witness Alberta William's opening stanza:

"I caught the tranp* truck
going north
leaving Florida behind, my three-year-old son
at my side.
It was June, and the celery was ripe
in upstate New York..."

The immense pathos these few lines suggests so economically represents one of the extraordinary pleasures of this anthology. The people here were migrants, as all Americans are migrants; moving here and then there and through the heartbreak and wonder that comes with being an American. Finally, to move, as Sarah McClellan says, toward that moment "when all the silence will make you sing." The members of this chorus come from the north and the south, are white and black, are Polish, Irish, Italian, German—a fair profile of our national identity.

Hard work beats out the rhythm of these lines that search and find life's joys in star shine, in the blessing of gladiolas, in the shine of new shoes. In a first kiss, still remembered. Here is love betrayed and love everstrong, and here, as well, are the hatreds and moral outrages of our century. For these are the lyrics of people of our time, pioneers as important as those who crossed the prairies in covered wagons but whose histories have been worn thin by films.

Ross Talarico has come across an unique lode of memory in Rochester, N.Y., and with utmost respect. "It's all a long journey," Mattie Whitley says, "the one that leads home." The marvelous quality of this collection is that at its conclusion lies a source of renewal, and refreshment.

HILARY MASTERS ∎

* tranp truck—term for migrant transportation truck

Introduction

AT THE HEART OF our affairs, there's a story—some time-intensified account of an event or encounter that shapes our perspective on life. It is, too often, a secret story, hidden in the cluttered corridors of memory. It is usually not a story that has been deliberately kept secret. On the contrary, it is often a story begging to be told...

Even if it is told, if the telling is without care and focus, a personal story often dissipates into the distorting air of its surroundings—the intrusions of the setting, the interruptions of dialogue, the distractions and mannerisms of storyteller and audience—until it serves not insight as much as confirmation of existing *attitudes*.

What I have tried to do in these oral history transcriptions is to give each its proper presentation, isolating each story so that its form on the page recreates the tone of the storyteller and the essence of the experience. Thus, the expression becomes a literary matter: the process of how the story unfolds is as essential as the story itself. And since these are all first-person narratives, there is an ennobling effect: each person's story is distinct, dignified. These people step out of anonymity, out of any stereotype—and into the unique light of universal character. The process changes one's view of another human being; therefore it changes all of us.

Transcribing these stories, I have come to appreciate and respect those who have taken the time (and in many cases the trouble) to reflect upon and articulate experiences from their pasts. Mattie Whitley, just before I completed writing her "Train Ride," called me at home to tell me how her soldier/husband sat with her on the train in Fort Worth and cried before she left him forever. It was, of course, a painful detail extracted at the very last moment only by the urgency of "getting the story right."

Earnst Radcliffe, before telling the story of his "Youth," insisted I meet with him privately, because the telling of his story brought tears to the eyes of this strong, hard-working man. "It ain't right for a man to cry in public," he said. Mamie "Mother" Haynes had never told the story of discovering the blood-stained clothes of her murderer-employers; she felt compelled to do so after experiencing and sharing the stories of others.

Ironically, oral history transcriptions were not originally a part of my plan when I initiated a grass-roots program in creative expression in Rochester, New York, in 1985. I began the program (which has had, I should add, phenomenal success and which has received national attention) to bring creative writing and language arts to those who had been left out of the process—people of all ages from all backgrounds and with differing levels of accomplishment. About six months after the program started, I received a call from a recreation-center director in charge of a program for elderly black women. She asked me what seemed at the time a very odd question: "Do you have to be able to read and write to be a part of the creative writing program?" Perhaps it was the apparent absurdity of the question that made me schedule a meeting with the Kennedy Tower senior citizen group the following Wednesday afternoon. Six years later, we are still meeting on Wednesday afternoons.

The term "oral history" was not even in my mind during that first meeting. I brought in a notebook and a few poems from my other senior citizens' writing groups to read to these women. I realized instantly that if I expected others to volunteer their personal stories, I'd better start by telling (not reading) a few of my own. Before long, I re-acquainted myself with some of life's basic truths—the stories that remain with us are usually love stories. In this case, first romances and marriages: Sarah McClellan's "First Marriage: A Ballad of Rain" was the first oral history discussed in that group, and it immediately set a pattern for interviewing.

We had fun as a group, probing for details in a non-threatening manner which made the storyteller uninhibited. Whatever reluctance there was gave way not only to the relaxed atmosphere, but to the urgency one feels when suddenly one's story begins to reveal itself before an accepting audience. Before long, the group deferred to the more detailed probing of the transcriber, and the tone of the related experiences affected the mood of the group itself. Ms. McClellan's story was followed by the tender romantic tale of one-hundred-and-one-year-old Texanna Sheppard's "Spring Vows." Romances were followed by stories of family deaths and personal losses.

Unlike most transcribers, I do not advocate the use of tape recorders except when necessary. As a writer, I rely on the intensity of my observations, a good ear to capture tone, as well as my ability to provide the questioning that will extract the details necessary for a vivid reconstruction of the experience. It is a good idea to hear the story several times—to note, for instance, the phrases that are repeated—such as Sarah McClellan's refrain "Every time it rained he went away..." (which the entire group began, spontaneously, to recite together once the story was underway), or Mattie Whitley's phrase "I wondered what he thought of me..." in her rendering of the poignant "Train Ride." A tape recorder, it seems to me, tends to flatten a story, affecting both narrator and writer. The narrator becomes too conscious of it as a storage receptacle for facts; the writer tends to be more journalistic and less sensitive to the re-creative elements of the writing experience. Transcriptions are mechanical by their nature and less selective than a poetic rendering requires. The story needs form and focus, and the art of oral histories necessitates a healthy partnership between storyteller and writer, each utilizing fully his individual skills, the final product a blend of substance, sensitivity and talent.

We are often disappointed and frustrated at the inability of our young people today to write, articulate or sometimes even form coherent ideas. And yet it is our culture these youngsters reflect with disturbing accuracy. Inundated with information, we are a people obsessed with list-making, trying to keep up with the storage capacities of the computer age—overwhelmed with quantity, and unsure of what comprises quality of experience. Consequently we seek shortcuts to express emotional responses to experiences that demand greater examination and focus. Three-minute music videos, cliche-ridden greeting cards, and hypnotic, repetitive television commercials serve as immediate shallow outlets for our feelings. Our authentic emotional responses, meanwhile, are buried. It becomes increasingly difficult to voice or even recognize them, even though they are essential to our sense of identity.

So the inability of young people to articulate unique and personal experience is not limited to their own generation: the individual stories of ordinary people of all ages are not being communicated in any meaningful manner. Significant moments in the lives of grandparents, parents, friends and even strangers die off with them. The death of each elderly person can be compared to a library burning down—nothing but ashes in the wind of an inarticulate heritage.

For me, the creation and publication of these oral history transcriptions marks the resurrection of an ancient role for the writer in the community. Someone with a story to tell unites with someone who can help to express that story to an audience. Lives open up and the experience of this grass-roots literature brings us closer together. The writer, so long considered to be a detached and mysterious figure, becomes relevant, respected and essential to a community intent on knowing itself through intimate revelation.

ROSS TALARICO, 1992 ■

Hearts and Times:
The Literature of Memory

Romance

First Marriage: A Ballad of Rain

WHEN EIGHTY-FOUR-YEAR-old Sarah McClellan was asked about her first romance and her first marriage, and how long it lasted, she answered with that characteristic twinkle in her eye, "Six months, and I always say five too long..." The other women around the table laughed as she told the story of that brief encounter, knowing of course how the foolishness of first love seems to last forever in the foolish heart—or in this case, almost seventy years! The story itself is universal: we fall in love for adventure, and sometimes for all the wrong reasons. But Sarah began her story—and continued it and eventually ended it—with the same refrain: "Every time it rained, he went away." She refers to the day off for a crop worker on a rainy day, a day to do other things. The refrain captures the ambiguity so often a part of first loves: *regret* that he leaves her, and at the same time, as we discover the danger of his character, *relief* that, indeed, he went away. ■

First Marriage: A Ballad of Rain
by Sarah McClellan

SOMETHING FUNNY ABOUT LEE.
Every time it rained
he went away.

Mama said don't,
he ain't your kind Sarah.
All he know
is to play that guitar
and skip into town...

And every time it rained
he went away...

It was raining and dreary
that day I agreed
to meet him in town.
He talked me into cutting my hair
and then he strummed his guitar
and smiled just so
and we got married, mama oh mama...

It lasted six months,
and I always say five too long.
We were given a cotton crop
to tend, and a
cabin all our own.

But Lee paid no mind,
and every time it rained
he went away.

The boss brought over
some hoes to be sharpened,
but Lee said
"What I know about filing a hoe?"

And he strummed his guitar,
and the wood pile vanished,
and the boss of that plantation
shook his head at our crop
and he didn't have
to say nothing about Lee
who every time it rained
he went away.

And one day
with the sun burning my mama's voice
deep down in my brain,
he never came back.
It seemed right to me
and I went back home.

A year later
on a rainy Fourth of July
he killed a man in another county.
I guess it's always raining
somewhere in Mississippi
and there was always some place
to take Lee away.

He wasn't my kind, though
I cut my hair for him.
He just do nothing
but strum on his guitar...

And every time it rained,
he went away.

Spring Vows

THERE WAS AN IMMEDIATE tenderness in the voice
and manner of one-hundred-and-one-year-old
Texanna Sheppard. There was this look on her
face—she had something to say about *romance*, and
(after a little coaxing) she was going to tell us her
story. It's an old story, almost ninety years old.
But it touches the universal core of all love sto-
ries—the simplicity of love, a time when it took
"about ten minutes" to pack the honeymoon lug-
gage, and cooking "fresh greens" was just about
fine for the wedding meal. Texanna kept saying,
as if it was still a mystery, "I guess he wanted me"—
expressing for all of us that mystery of attraction
that so often defies understanding. When Robert
holds her in his arms, Texanna feels like cotton:
white, pure, as light as the spirit that makes her say
with such lovely conviction almost a hundred
years later, "We had everything we needed." ■

Spring Vows
Texanna Sheppard

1904

DOWN IN GREENVILLE
eighty-some long years ago
by the spring that ran through
the Henson plantation,
I saw the preacher awaiting,
leaning on the old bridge,
and Robert in his clean new overalls
giving him a dollar
as the sun fell a little
in that Alabama sky.

We had everything there,
cotton, corn, cane and beets,
but Robert had no family
and I guess he wanted me.
I was nineteen
and he was older, forty-some I reckon,
and he spent his days
working the good road, six mules
to a grader, twenty men
to a mile.
Some days he'd weigh cotton at the warehouse.
But I guess he wanted me.

My aunt got our license
in one of her trips to town.
She was the only one to know.
I told my ma I was going
to wash out the clothes at the spring
like always.
I did not say it was my marrying day.
The preacher was in a hurry
and didn't waste any words.

We didn't even kiss when it was over,
or should I say
when it all began.

Robert went back to his place
to gather collard greens,
and said he'd come over in a day or two
to tell my ma.
I went home, feeling good all over,
and I was sweeping the backyard
when I spied Robert
making his way up to my mama
who was sitting on the porch steps.
"I come down to get my wife," he said.
"You're not married," said Mama, kindly.
"Yes they is," said my aunt
peeking through the screen door.

It took about ten minutes
to pack my bag.
At Robert's place we stuffed
the bed with cotton.
We cooked fresh greens and after a while
we gave each other a kiss or two.
The moon shone over us
and we sent out a little sigh to that
Alabama sky.
Robert held me so carefully,
just like he was weighing cotton.
And even that first night of our marriage
we had everything we needed.

Train Ride

MATTIE WHITLEY'S "TRAIN RIDE" is surely an excursion through romance—through hope, infatuation, loneliness and despair. The many states through which she travels reflect the many states of mind she experiences in this tale of her long-distance love affair. Tommy Ross remains, symbolically, somewhat of a stranger throughout their brief but drawn-out encounters, just as love itself appears and disappears in many people's lives without warning or explanation. Mattie kept repeating her refrain in this poem, "I wondered what he thought of me," and I understood that was a question that she, like all of us, would take to her grave—still "in love" despite the failure of her marriage to Tommy Ross. "The high altitude gives me a headache," says Mattie, referring literally to the Wyoming setting of the quixotic wedding. But it's the metaphor that strikes our own lives as well; the spiritual "high" we experience falling in love often leaves us with pain. Mattie's own story and its subsequent poem have been favorites of mine and others, probably because, as Mattie concludes, "It's all a long journey, the one that leads home." And that's where we'd like to harbor those deep feelings that come from such travels. ■

Train Ride
Mattie Whitley

I. Atlanta to Wyoming

CHOO, CHOO, CLICKETY HISS...
I'm on a train, heading west.

He's a soldier in Wyoming,
and he sounds as lonely as me.
I read through another of his letters
as the train thumps on.
Chattanooga, Sewanee, Clarksville, Paducah...
the porter calls out.
I keep his photo at my side, looking so tall in his
uniform;
I wonder what he'll think of me?

His name is Tommy Ross,
and I found him listed in the *Pittsburgh Courier*, a
colored paper
we get in Atlanta.
I just picked his name and wrote,
and he wrote back.
Six months of letters and then
the invitation to the base in Wyoming.
I took two weeks from the work I do,
cook and nursemaid
and lately what seems just a sentimental fool.
Jonesboro, Red Bud, East St. Lou...

In the bag I packed
I carry two dresses, always do,
one black, just in case,
and another the prettiest, prettiest blue.
I carry a Bible,
and read myself to hope and sleep.
The porter brings some hot tea,

no coloreds in the dining car.
But there are stars galore in the western skies,
and I pick one out and
give it a wish, like everyone else
traveling so far.
I wonder what he'll think of me.

II. *Laramie, Wyoming*

Kansas City, Atchinson, Broadwater, Cheyenne...
I'm coming just as fast, and just
as slow as I can.
Choo, choo, clickety hiss...
I'm on this train and heading west.

...Before I know it, there he is.
On the platform, so handsome, and even
taller than his picture,
taking my bag, my arm, and I'm
still wondering what he thinks of me.
At the barracks he drops off my things
and shows me my letters in a duffel bag.
At the cafe in the servicemen's club
I meet a hundred soldiers
and they all call me Mattie, like they've
known me all the while.

Turns out Tommy Ross, he's got
everything arranged—time off, an apartment
on base for the two of us,
a dance arranged that night at
the servicemen's club,
and, after a night of holding me
in his strong arms,
an invitation to marry him that week.

"You joking?" I say,
and he just nods his head, and then

I nod mine.
The high altitude gives me a headache,
and I think it's never going to leave,
even as the chaplain is asking
whether I do or whether I dare;
and when I'm kissing Tommy Ross
and later dancing in his arms in my blue dress,
and seeing the soldiers acting so crazy
toasting us so on that joyful night,
the headache stays, like a nagging memory,
and all the happiness in the world
can't shake it.

When the two weeks is over
he takes me back to the depot.
I watch him wave from the platform
and I close my eyes for a longer goodbye.
Already the porter is calling out
his song of destinations,
Northport, Grand Island, Boonville, St. Lou...
Choo, choo, clickety hiss...
I'm on this train, heading east.
We said soon we'd be together,
but it wouldn't turn out that way.
Marion, Nashville, Chattanoo...
In Tennessee my head got better,
but not my heart.
I read through a batch of letters, and I
looked at the photo that now would never do.
Choo, choo, clickety hiss...
I closed my eyes and remembered his kiss.
I was a married woman, and yet,
how could it be:
I still kept wondering what he thought of me.

III. Germany, Ft. Worth, Texas, and Atlanta

Six months later, without us ever

visiting again, he was sent to Germany.
The letters were slow, so slow,
I'd pray...
There was so much, so little to say.
I was a married woman,
but no man around.
I was a cook and a nursemaid
and a sentimental fool. Again the photo
was all I had; even Wyoming
seemed like a cool mountain dream.
For two years I waited
for some kind of news, my heart full,
the headache nagging with its memory.
And before I knew it, the war all over,
I got a letter from Oklahoma, and Tommy Ross
saying he was being discharged, that he
was going home, and to get on that train
and meet him in Fort Worth in Texas.

Choo, choo, clickety hiss...
I'm on this train again, heading west.
Two bags this time,
and just in case, two dresses,
one black, the other the prettiest of blues.
Tuscaloosa, Biloxi, New Orleans, Port Arthur...
I really didn't know what to do,
apart so long, three years older,
all that loneliness behind us.
I was still a wondering what he thought of me.

And we were happy for a month or two.
Conceived a child in fact,
but it must've been bad blood, because
one night it began to flow,
and I guess it emptied both of us,
and another night Tommy Ross didn't come
home.
And then another. And then one more.

I could already hear the porter
calling out in my mind: *Galveston, Baton Rouge...*

And sure enough, a month later
I was standing on the platform
at the depot in Ft. Worth, the sky
so dark and heavy
but me in my dress, the loneliest of blues.
And on the train he sat with me awhile,
before the blast of the whistle
and the choo choo and the clickety hiss
of this old train heading back east.

He said he didn't need nothing
and then he cried.
He told the porter to take care of me
Because I had just miscarried and was
short of strength.
When he left he stopped on the platform
as the train began to move.
He waved like he did in Wyoming.
And I closed my eyes the same way...
Mobile, Georgianna, Tallapoosa, Atlanta...

It's all a long journey, the one
that leads home.
I carried a Bible, two dresses, a photo...
I carried my love, whatever the pain,
and when the porter says *Heaven*, and
gives me his hand,
I'll shake my head kindly, and tell him not yet,
and I'll head on to Atlanta, where
the sun starts to rise,
where the light falls so briefly, oh Lord,
and forms your beautiful tears in my eyes.

Convertible, 1928

KATHERYN EDELMAN'S STORY IS so American in nature. It's about a spirit that soars despite the toughest of times, the Depression years. The metaphor, so apt, is the automobile, a convertible no less, that speeds down the highway even though the young broke couple do not know exactly where they are going. I was amazed to hear this story from this relatively poor, eighty-four-year-old woman whose romance had to do with a defiant sense of herself and a brand new Hudson automobile. I remember the sheer delight on everyone's face as she revealed her "irresponsible" act—buying the car right out of the showroom with the mortgage money. All those of us who know Katheryn and her poem (it was published in our Sunday magazine), will always picture her behind the wheel of that convertible, "top down eighty miles an hour," her baby strapped to the seat, pushing her foot to the floor. It's a part of the American Dream—and she lived it for a brief while, God bless her. ■

Convertible, 1928
Katheryn Edelman

TOP DOWN, EIGHTY MILES an hour,
dust rising
through the apple-scented air
of Route 104,
little George strapped down
to the brown leather cushions
of the front seat,
I aimed that Hudson toward Syracuse
and pushed my foot to the floor...

I saw the car
white top up one day, down the next,
in a showroom on Stone Street
in Rochester.
Every day I walked by it,
seeing myself behind the wheel,
my sunlit hair in the wind.
When I told my husband I wanted it,
he said simply, "Buy it."
But he didn't say it joyfully or eagerly.
There was a kind of resignation
in his voice;
he had wanted to go to Europe
with the money we had—I'd wanted
a house, and that's
what we bought a year earlier.

So I scraped up all the money
I could get my hands on,
about twelve hundred dollars
(including the mortgage money)
and I drove that Hudson convertible
right out of the showroom.
When I drove it around the neighborhood,
my friends thought I was a bootlegger's wife.

I took weekly trips to my mother
in Syracuse,
and I let the wind
have its way with my hair.

But the broker didn't hesitate
when our mortgage was late,
and in thirty days past due
there were locks on the doors,
and the house my husband never wanted
wasn't ours anymore.
He got laid off too,
being the Depression and all.
Europe was even more distant in his eyes.

So we made our way
to my mom's farm in Syracuse,
where we had to live for awhile.
Broke, we drove around
in that Hudson convertible
until even little George learned to
laugh in the modest glory
of the rumble seat.
On Route 104 there were no speed laws,
no cops,
and we drove so stylishly fast,
like a bootlegger and a bootlegger's wife.
But we were a little scared then,
not of the speed,
but because we didn't know exactly
where we were going.

Youth

No, Earnst Radcliffe wouldn't tell his story in front of others, embarrassed somehow by the tears he knew he would shed reliving his encounters with his stepfather, his wife and her family, and his real father. "Seems like I was always leaving somewhere," says Radcliffe, "counting the money in my pockets." Just seventy-five cents, as a matter of fact, when he ran away from home as a young boy after protecting his brother from an ax-swinging step-pa. When we take the time to reflect upon our lives, we focus on the touchstones of our experience, those moments which seemed to give our lives direction, for better or for worse. In Radcliffe's "Youth," there are, I believe, the elements of a novel—the initiations into manhood, the sexual pursuit, the fall from grace, and the life-affirming encounter with beauty (the gladiola farm) that somehow becomes the complement to a life rising out of the ashes of dejection. As I wrote from the several pages of notes from his interview, I was astonished how the pieces fell together. It should have hit me, though, from the beginning: a man who feels the tears welling within is the right man to tell his story! ∎

Youth

Earnst Radcliffe

1. Waterboro, South Carolina

I WAS THIRTEEN, MAYBE fourteen,
the day my brother LeRoy played hookey
and, though he should've known better,
took our step-parents' grocery money
and gambled it away
with those boys in the north woods.
"Don't cry," I told him
when he came to me, "I'll get the money
back..."

But they wouldn't give it back,
and when we told our step-pa
it all happened so fast
I don't remember the words, and when
I close my eyes
I see it happening again, like I'm watching
an old movie that keeps getting
clearer with age:

My step-pa's so angry
he tosses his cap and grabs on
to the axe he's chopping wood with.
He turns toward me
but it's LeRoy burning in his eyes,
and with one wild heave
of that heavy oak-handled axe
he moves toward my brother
and starts to swing....
I picked up whatever was close,
a short oak log with a
couple of sharp branches sticking out.
And I heaved it with all
the strength and accuracy of my fear,

hitting my step-pa right square
on the side of the head,
and he went down dropping his arms,
the axe, the blood spurting
from his temple like a stream.
I stared at the fallen man, unconscious,
just laying there. LeRoy standing over him,
then looking at me.
"Take care of him," I said, scared I might
have killed him.
"Call an ambulance," I said to LeRoy,
who looked at me with such a mixture
of love and fright I'll never forget.
"I'm gone," I added, taking
a couple of steps backward, then
a few more, until I ran all the way
to the bus station in town.

I had seventy-five cents in my pocket,
and got off in Savannah, Georgia.
I had an uncle there named Dog.
I climbed a fence
and found an open cab of a Royal Crown
truck,
and fell asleep.
In the morning some guy woke me up,
but he wasn't angry.
He said I could ride deliveries with him,
and later he asked, "Want a job?"
It made me feel pretty good,
but my belly still ached, and my mind still
hurt.

2. Daytona Beach

First the cigarette fell from Simon Fry, the
regular cook's mouth,
then old Simon himself, who drank

more than he ought to, fell flat on his face
behind the stove one day, dead drunk.
And that's when I took up
the fry station, turning all that meat
on the steaming grill.

I was fifteen,
with a lot of faith in God,
and a job in the cafeteria baking
cornbread, biscuits, and potato pie.
Now, frying meat not only
paid better, there were other benefits:
I could eat free,
and more important, I could trade meat
for dates with the waitresses.
And that's how I met Winnie Ruth
a year or so later.
Before long we made our way to Nero's,
a transit room
where you could pay a buck and a quarter
and make love for a hour.
And the second time we went, I swear,
she got in the family way.
And before I knew it, we had four boys,
a good marriage, and a bunch of in-laws
that took half the money I made
laying cables for Bell Telephone.

Winnie Ruth still liked making love
and having babies; the more she fed me,
the poorer I got.
So I was probably looking for an excuse
when my real father, A. L. Radcliffe, wrote
me
and said he was sick, and wanted
to see his oldest son, and to come down
to Greensville right quick.

When I got there
the moonshine was flowing.
My daddy wasn't sick, just a little
too happy for his own good.
I drank too,
and when some dude named Jake
slapped my daddy during an argument,
I started a fight with him,
and before I knew it
I ripped a small potato knife I had
from my cooking days
against the flesh over his ribs.
So that night, in Greensville for less
than twenty-four hours, to keep peace
between two families,
I had to leave town, for good.

In Daytona, Winnie and her family wanted
no part of me, claiming I'd fallen
from sugar to you know what.
I slept under the stars that night,
thinking back to that Royal Crown truck
in Savannah a few years earlier.
It seemed like I was always
hurting someone hoping to save someone
else,
like I was always leaving family somewhere,
counting the money in my pockets.

3. Going North

His name was Cannonball,
and I didn't believe for a minute
that his old Pontiac
would make it to Savannah—not Georgia,
where I would have been happy to go—
but Savannah, New York, up north.
But what choice did I have?

So I climbed in
and listened to him talk for miles on end
about gladiolas—how to plant
and care for them,
and when we got there
I pressed those seeds gently into the dirt,
like I was paying my dues
to the good fresh earth.
And a few months later, standing in
the midst of such colors under the clear
blue sky,
I clipped those gladiolas, their scent
rising from the huge meadow of perfume,
each bouquet, hundreds of them,
a strange blessing to a difficult life.

The Proposal

A COUPLE OF YEARS ago I convinced the ABC television affiliate station in Rochester to produce "poetry videos" of poems and oral histories to promote the city's creative writing program. One of them was Rose Muscarella's "Proposal." The images from old photos and news clippings, along with the sixty-plus-year-old photos of Rose and her new husband Joe, remain with me still. There's a simplicity in this poem—the matrimonial walk past an America that offers its goods—furniture, cars, etc —as if they were as natural as the blossoms of trees and rosebushes. There is a sense of belonging, a feeling of being one with everything around her—so it is the world around her that answers, yes, yes, when Joe, to whom she'll be wed for more than sixty years, makes his proposal. ■

The Proposal
Rose Muscarella

WHAT I LIKE IS walking in the
moonlight, listening to
the echo of distant traffic,
feeling my heart beat faster,
and thinking it's great to be alive....

1925
The Rialto Theatre on East Avenue.
Sun shining on a Saturday afternoon,
we walked from Bay Street and Eighth,
my house, and halfway there, about
two or three miles I guess, Joe put his arm
around me.
I'd known him about a year,
but this was the first time we were
allowed to go somewhere by ourselves,
just the two of us, though I had
to be back by dark.
We passed the beautiful lawns of the
East Avenue mansions, the museum
and all its history inside,
the splendor of the George Eastman House,
roses blossoming along the trellis
in the courtyard;
and nearer downtown, Reuben's furniture store
where we looked in and saw a beautiful
polished maple dining set.
And Hallman's Chevrolet, Joe's eyes
gleaming like new paint;
and the stately RG&E building.
We watched the traffic,
dreaming of our own adventures.

And after the movie,
when Joe asked me to marry him,

I heard the street whisper yes, yes.
The blue sky too whispered yes.
And of course I said it too.

Over The Years

WHAT I CAN'T PASS on to the reader is the look in Louella Red's eyes when she reminisced about X.L. Butler, the boy she had fallen in love with sixty years earlier. When she said that a proposal from him now would make her legs "right" so that she could walk out of the senior citizen residence, those of us sitting with her certainly could feel the power of love. Louella's story reminds us not only of the romantic infatuation universal among young people, but of its power in an environment of hardship and difficult times. She remembers the long walks to borrow a bucket of meal, the image of X.L. chopping cotton with a hoe—and even being "switched" across her back by a brutally strict mother. But Louella's unrequited love, which lights up her face, is the focus of her story. Her image of X.L. on his horse, "white shirt, black tie, the belt hanging just so on the back of his jacket," is as vivid and classical a portrait as Louella herself as she gazes out toward a scene we too can glimpse. And his wave reflects that eternal ambiguity of love kept alive in the stubborn heart: "Hello" to the dreamer, "Goodbye" to the sad but appreciative realist. ■

Over The Years
Louella Red

I WISH I COULD have melted away
in his arms that night, sixty-some
years ago, as the warm
Mississippi breeze blew across the porch
and our eyes met and knees touched
under the early evening shadow
of my mama's eyes.

And today, if Mr X.L. Butler
would come to me,
brushing off the dust of
all those years, and if he would say
"Would you marry me, Miss Louella?"
I believe my legs would right themselves
and I'd get up
and walk right out of here by his side...

X.L.'s horse had a habit
of coming over and neighing
and pawing so with its hoof at the door,
and Mama would start searching
the house and yard, and saying
"Louella, you hiding that boy somewhere?"
And sometimes X.L. did come over
but not too often and only for
a few minutes or so.
But that big old horse came over
more than he did.
Once in a while, he'd make plans
to come over and court,
sitting on the porch till nine o'clock,
my mother sitting there across from us,
eyeing us so.
The only time I could sneak a kiss
was when I'd get him his hat to go.

On Friday nights, I'd dress all out
for the church choir recitals.
X.L. directed the choir, his father,
being the Baptist preacher and all.
And since Mama made me wear
a wrapped black stocking over my hair
all during the week at school,
I wanted X.L. to take
some special notice on Friday nights,
not just notice of my voice,
but of me...I mean all of me.
I wore a snake hip dress,
long and shapely, tight over my hips,
and falling so lady-like over my shoes.

I was eleven when we met,
and about seventeen when he made
those visits to my front porch.
Maybe it was the times,
or the years, or just me, or maybe
my mama's strict ways,
like the time she switched me so
across my back
when instead of going over to Miss Giles
to borrow a bucket of meal,
I took a wander along Willow Tree Lake,
hoping to run into X.L. across the fields
where he chopped cotton with a hoe.
That was 1925, and nothing much
happened for a while, except
my love for X.L. burning so,
until 1939 when he went off and
married Inez, that knotty-head girl
who must have earned the grace of God
somewhere along the road,
but not in my mind.
The day I found out I packed my bags
and took off for Shaw, Mississippi,

and then, some years later,
made my way here to upstate New York.

I can still see X.L.,
white shirt and black tie, the belt
hanging just so on the back of his jacket,
as he rode that white horse—
that same horse that appeared at our door
more times than his master—
as he rode on Sundays over the hills
and through the flickering sunlight
between the trees of the lovely
landscape of my dreaming days.
He'd wave to me
and in return I'd wish him my love.
I always thought of that wave
as a welcoming, a sweet hello
from the distance,
but maybe he was just saying goodbye
as beautifully as he knew how.

Initiations

The Mansion

SOME STORIES TAKE MANY years to tell. And although
I had the feeling that Helen Johnson was finally
telling the story of her childhood to others, it was
obvious that the pain in her voice and in her
expression had been a part of her existence for a
long, long time. Helen Johnson's story recounts the
unspoken moments of a generation, the hidden
abuses and the fearful silences of a broken family.
Her metaphor, the exterior of a beautiful house,
represents the grand illusion, the prospering fami-
ly. Her temporary friends (the family moved so
often) admire the mansion, but cannot enter with-
out risk of exposing the emptiness not simply of
rooms, but of Helen herself. She protects her moth-
er by locking the oak door of the bathroom, know-
ing of course her father would not destroy *it*! At
the end of the poem, mother and daughter huddle
together by the fading fire, abandoned but now
safe in each other's arms. ■

The Mansion

Helen Johnson

MY FATHER WAS A carpenter
and I can see him standing
in the streaks of light
touching the gumwood trim
in the newly finished sun parlor.
I can see my mother
holding her hands over the small fire
burning like a stray thought
in the massive brick fireplace.
I see myself
leaning against the leaded glass
of the doors that lead
to the library, the shelves empty of course,
and my vision
a rainbow of confusion...

There was no furniture
except some old crates and mattresses.
I made up stories
to keep my friends out
as they walked home from school
and stopped to admire
the stately mansion they called my home.
But it was temporary.
Soon the house was sold, and we moved on,
my father packing his tools.
For a few months we lived well,
enough coal to heat the half-built rooms,
chicken, dried carrots, cabbage
and pierogi.
But before long, as the house took shape,
and the walls were plastered,
and the fireplaces bricked, and
the doors fitted with bronze hardware,
it was back to noodles and rice.

And that would have been all right
except for the beatings
and the cold stare of my father
who seemed to love his work
but not his life.
I remember locking a bathroom door
with my mother inside
and hiding the key, and my father
pounding on the door
as he had often pounded on her.
But he would not destroy
such a rich finished oak door.

One day he dragged a steamer trunk
into the barren vestibule
and onto the front porch.
Badz zdrowa, he said, without any emotion
at all; it means, in Polish, *stay well*.
And when a small pickup truck
pulled up, and he got in,
that's the last we saw of him.
We looked at each other,
at the sparseness of the huge room,
of our lives to that point,
and we held onto each other
until the fire went out.

Mount Rushmore

HARRY NOLLSCH SOUNDS AS if he works for the South Dakota Chamber of Commerce. He still wears a Western string tie. It's obvious that he loves his home state, but in his recollections Harry tended to leave himself out of his stories, as if he were merely an observer. It's a common notion that the history of a place is somehow divorced from personal history. One function of literature, as I see it, is to tie character to place, experience to event. That must have been an eerie feeling when the faces on Mount Rushmore seemed a little more distinct each day as this teenage boy tried to discover himself. Harry finally relented under our questioning, recalling an old girlfriend, the camaraderie of swims in the irrigation ditch and as much as we could get about his father and the tough life of a Western rancher in those days. I like the levels of expression in Harry's story, the lighter memories fused with the deeper contemplations, both forming, like the September wind, the character who feels, under the half-emerged portraits of heroes on Rushmore, the expression still forming on his own face. ■

Mount Rushmore

Harry Nollsch

I CAN'T BEGIN TO tell you
how strange it is
to see a face emerge, one feature
at a time, from a distance
only a young boy knows,
there in South Dakota in the Thirties,
among the stretches of cropland,
tied to the river of time
by the brown waters
of the irrigation ditch and good friends.

As an old man now
I go back, visiting George, the
other half of the graduating class
of 1933 at the little country school
we attended in the Western plains.
He now lives in the place
my folks occupied when I left for
the service in 1942.
He takes me into the tiny room
between the ice shed and the house
where I slept as a kid, and he
points to a dusty shelf, one I remember
building over my bed more than
fifty years ago.
Still visible, the two hearts I
carved there, one with an *H*, the other
with an *E*....

I think back to Skyline Drive
overlooking Rapid City
below me and the girl next to me
in a '36 Plymouth; the lights seem to
reach for miles. Even the glow
of Ellsworth Air Force Base offers

its promise of a country waiting.
I look up north to the darkness
surrounding Mount Rushmore, thinking
maybe the eyes of those four great men
close at night, like ours,
and maybe they too dream, like we do,
of a vast country filled with
adventure and love...

George tells me the young girl
in my mind is now a great-grandmother
living in a town some thirty miles away.
I wonder what we might say
to each other, what anyone says really,
after all these years.
I remind George of the irrigation ditch,
which would bring water to
the fields of sugar beets, corn, and
cucumbers, and where we'd go
on those September evenings for a
"last swim" of the season, the moon
rising from behind the willow trees
as we rode our horses
out over the Dakota plains.
The moonlight would dance on the
little waves and miniature whirlpools
in the dark brown water of the ditch,
as we'd strip off our clothes
and jump into the ditch, incredibly happy.

I don't know, in fact,
how my father managed those days;
our farm was "dry," we had to rely on
natural rainfall, my father forced
to mortgage his livestock or farm machinery
to tide us over until another harvest.
How he ever fed us during
these times I'll never know.   As a

matter of fact, gas always being
in short supply, we only made it once
to Mount Rushmore, seeing the faces
of Washington and Jefferson, and the
half-completed face of Roosevelt
slowly emerging in the midst
of such a barren and beautiful America.
Lincoln's face, his stern resolve,
was still a dream in the stone carver's
strong hands. From that day on
I took some time to stare out
across the miles at those four great men,
and to meditate on my own achievements.

I run my weathered hand, still sensitive
to the touch, over the initialed hearts
in my old room, hardly big enough,
I reflect, for a wish or two, let alone
the contemplation of a lifetime.
I know I'll never make it out to the ditch
again, and feel the cool, life-giving
water under the moonlight.
But no matter where I stand, half
of me in South Dakota, half in memory,
I'm under the gaze of those
four men atop Mount Rushmore,
and I'll think about my own contribution
to a life of hard work, decency,
minor but wonderful adventures,
and of course whatever romance one can find.
And I'll stand back, the confidence
only an old man knows, feeling
that old September wind after a last swim
as we rode our tired horses back home,
that cold autumn wind, like
a sculptor's hands,
forming the expression on my face.

Silver Dollars, Silver Memories

OLD STORIES BRING US back—not just to another time
and place, but often back to values that define the
American character. Darlene Bargmann's story
reminds us of hard times, loving families, and var-
ious ethnic groups struggling together to get by.
She fills her story with vivid details; we see the
cold-water flat, smell the German sauerkraut, and
hear the jingle of the silver dollars in the coffee can
hidden in the closet. I wrote a line of poetry one
day—"Close your eyes and take a good look at
me." That's what happens when a good storyteller
captures us; once we see what our mind imagines,
the image is as powerful as one on a movie screen
—more powerful because we, with the storyteller,
are co-creators. This story brings us back to a time
in America worth reliving. This is a Christmas
story as well (it was published on Christmas Day
in our Gannett newspaper in Rochester) which
reaffirms the notion that poignant stories remind
us not only of times, but of hearts. The silver dol-
lar recovered that Christmas Eve is a symbol of the
simple but universal love we spend our days try-
ing to recover. ∎

Silver Dollars, Silver Memories

Darlene Bargmann

EVERY YEAR WHEN MY mother had a child, my father gave her a silver dollar. So she had eight silver dollars. Can you believe that my entire childhood was spent borrowing these silver dollars and getting them back...

My mother was born in 1889 in Montana. My father was born ten years earlier than that in Michigan, and somehow made his way to Butte, Montana and married my mother. But there was no work in Montana, so my father went off to find work. "Go any place and I'll follow— any place but New York City," my mother said to my father as he left. So I'm here to tell you that he went right to New York City and found work as a barber!

Mom arrived with us at a cold-water flat in Brooklyn. There was plumbing, but no hot water—just a coal stove in the kitchen where you could heat up water in the back. The tenement houses were usually about six stories high—and since the farther up the less expensive the flats, I want to tell you that we always lived on the top floor.

No, my mom didn't like it, but she knew she'd never have enough money to move back to Montana, so she said if she had to stay there, she'd make it the best life she could. And she did. Those were the days of large families, the days when moms were home. I remember how happy I was to climb the stairs past the floors of all the families—especially in the afternoons when all the cooking was being done. I can still remember the aroma of the pasta from the Italian family on the second floor, and the German sauerkraut on the third floor, and the sausage from the Polish family under us. We got along and there was a warm feeling of belonging that we all shared.

On the top floor, our flat, everyone crowded in on Saturday nights. We were not, let me tell you, a quiet family. My father played the mandolin, my brother Bob the guitar, Billy the banjo, and my brother Lou the saxophone. They would play and everyone would keep rhythm and sing along. I remember my mother putting pillows under our feet as we kept to the music, trying to keep the noise down. But there were times when neighbors tapped broom handles on the ceiling to complain. Funny, we didn't have much, but we were a together family, a loving family.

No, my mother would never get back to Montana, but she left me the most wonderful inheritance I believe possible to bequeath a child—because she knew how to love, how to make you feel so good. She knew how to mother children—and I've certainly put that to good use in my life.

I was the last born, in 1930. I was the

eighth silver dollar. My mother had a can, a coffee or cocoa can I believe. She didn't believe in banks (and we had nothing to keep in a bank!). And she'd hammer this can into the floor of the closet wherever we lived (and we moved often, let me tell you). In that can she kept the silver dollars my father gave her for each child that was born. I don't know how she thought that would keep the silver dollars from being stolen, but that was her idea. They were her prized possessions.

All of us knew how important these silver dollars were to her. She'd get out an old rag and polish them and then start to tell the stories behind them—who was there when the child was born, what the times were like, what the weather had been, if the child were early or late.... I can't tell you the times Mama and Papa took out those silver dollars and the stories that would unfold when they began talking about them. As a matter of fact, the stories seemed to grow as the years went by—more and more details emerged; so I guess they were storytellers after all, just like I am now.

We were our own bank. We felt somehow we were rich with our silver dollars—*eight* silver dollars! When times would get rough, we'd take a silver dollar out of our "bank," the can in the closet, and we'd buy some groceries and tell the grocery man to save the silver dollar and we'd buy it back. I can't tell you how

many times we bought back those silver
dollars!

Now I'll tell you one story about those
silver dollars. It was December. I was
born in the middle of the Depression, and
I was about four or five, so it must have
been around 1934. We had no money,
and like others were having a tough time
financially. My mother made many things
we needed to live, including gifts for
Christmas. But we were very poor that
year.

So we took a silver dollar to the grocery
store and asked him to hold it and we'd
buy it back. He was a jolly old Italian man
with a mustache and a big white apron
and a straw hat, and he always did this
willingly. In those times grocers and
others had to create their own systems of
credit and trust so everyone could survive.
That was early December. We had
another silver dollar out at the same time
—with the man who sold the bags of coal
we needed to warm the flat.

On my way home from school one day,
the grocer stopped me and said that if my
mama wanted that silver dollar, she'd
better get me the money right away —
"causa I a canta hold onto it mucha
longer," he said in his thick Italian accent.

We took odd jobs and tried everything to
earn money to buy back that silver dollar.
We did manage to buy back the one from
the coal man because we needed another

bag of coal that cold December. But
there was still this one silver dollar out.
My mama said maybe we just had to let it
go because she wanted us to have a little
something for Christmas (she had been
sewing for days).

My mother, by the way, was the woman
people called to help them when a baby
was about to be born. She was popular
because she had a hand-held scale. So if
you didn't have Mama there when you
had your baby, you wouldn't know how
much your baby weighed. You'd have to
wrap up your baby and go to the grocery
store. So Mama was immensely popular.
That December, the Italian family in the
building called Mama. They were a nice
family, fun and warm, and of course
didn't have much to give, like us.

Meanwhile, we thought we had lost that
silver dollar, and it was ruining our
holiday.

Every time I walked past the grocery store
my heart was in my feet cause I felt so
awful. It was December 24th, Christmas
Eve, and I'll never forget this. The Italian
man whose baby my mother helped
deliver gave my mother a box of
chocolate cherries, and on the top of the
box was a dollar bill!

Well, let me tell you, several of my
brothers and sisters took that folded
dollar bill and ran to the grocery store.
The man was just about to close. When

we walked in with the dollar bill he was so happy to see us and gave us that silver dollar. And I'll never forget this: he wouldn't take the folding money, the dollar bill, and he handed it back to us and said, "Merry Christmas, children."

Time went on, and our family prospered, but my mother always had those silver dollars. As she got older, they meant a great deal to her. When she went into a nursing home, she had to take them with her, and sad to say, I visited her one day and someone had stolen five of her silver dollars. It was, oh my, such a terrible feeling.

I bought five silver dollars and replaced them in the nursing home, and my mother never knew they were missing.

But I did take the ones that she still had from my father, and took the three coins to a jeweler and now have a beautiful long necklace with the three remaining silver dollars. But I certainly have those wonderful silver memories of my wonderful parents, and those stories they wove into my childhood that can never be lost and never be stolen—because they're a great inheritance.

The White Children

WHEN LUVEGIA HAMILTON SPOKE the words that begin her story, I wrote them down, underlined them, marked them with an asterisk. It isn't often a thematic statement comes so clearly to the lips of the storyteller. This *was* a story about fear—the intimidation of young black kids by whites. But to hear Luvegia tell it—to see her eyes and the proud look on her face, she was expressing more about dignity and strength of character than anger and resentment. Yes, hers was a daily routine, an indoctrination of sorts. If there was any hope for an integrated country, it came at times when least expected—white and black youth not being able to resist the cool, refreshing waters of Lake Seminole, when, as Luvegia tells us in her lyrical voice, "all that nature made us forget who we were..." ■

The White Children
Luvegia Hamilton

WE LEARNED EARLY ON
not to show the fear on our faces.
It was a long walk, every day
from Woodbridge to our school
in Eatonville, two and one-half miles or so.
We'd have to pass Maitland,
where the white school was,
and almost every day they'd
come up to us, taunt us, push us,
slap us, call us names, and make us
get out of the way.

We'd always group walk,
clowning, having fun, walking
the rails till we fell off...
Until we came to the white school,
when we'd quiet up,
and get out of the path if
someone was walking it.
Once, Verdell's cousin from Georgia
was visiting and didn't know enough
to move out of the way of a white kid.
We knew there'd be trouble.

And sure enough, the next day
the police met us, warning us
to stay out of the way for the white kids
to pass, to step out of the dirt rut
we was walking in. The parents
of the white kids were there too,
yelling names at us and telling us
they'd take us to the middle of the lake
if we didn't behave, all the while
the police nodding their heads.

Finally, a cousin, Mr. Banks, who
worked for the white lawyer,
came by and told the police to
let us go, and after a few
more minutes of threats, we were
allowed to make our way to school.
When we arrived late, our teacher,
young Mr. Richardson,
gave each of us five licks
on the hand for being late.

But even Mr. Richardson himself
had to take the walk through town
past the white school
after tutoring some old folks
near Woodbridge. And I'm not sure
what happened, who stopped him
and what they said,
but from that day on
he didn't give us licks any more
if we showed up late.

Once in a while, at Lake Seminole,
we'd swim all day, and sometimes
white kids would stay in the water
even when we jumped in.
Seems like all that nature
made us forget who we were....
But on our way to school, almost
two miles into our walk,
a quiet would come about
as we saw the white school in
the distance.
We grouped closer, stuck our heads
high in the air, and walked
with no fear on our faces, and our
hearts beat soundly like ancient drums.

The Last Race

BOB HASLIP'S MEMORY SOUNDS like a child's fantasy, a *Lassie* episode—and sometimes we forget that is exactly what life offers us. I feel a kind of envy when I read this story because it is truly an adventure I'd like to have experienced. I especially like the setting: the run-down training track, the old hands who surely had their own moments of glory there in the dust-filled skies of their own histories. There's a certain grace here, and we feel it, I believe, when the young boy begins to enjoy his perilous ride—simple, adventuresome, good-natured moments such as this one are so hard to come by. ■

The Last Race
Bob Haslip

ST. MARY WAS STILL a beautiful horse,
that 21-year-old mare, her
brown coat no longer shiny and smooth,
but elegantly speckled with gray.
Her back was swayed a bit,
but she still stood tall.
Her eyes were clouded, near blind
she was, though I imagine she saw what
she wanted to see, for she
maintained the stature of a proud champion.

My cousin and I stood in the pasture,
as we did often there in the
farm country of upstate New York, at
my uncle Arthur's training track in Hilton.
It was 1932. I was twelve or so,
and we often spent time up the hill
in the pasture with the old horses who
were treated kindly by my uncle.
We hooked a rope to the halter of
St. Mary as we had done before,
and I hopped on, pleading
with the animal to move a bit.

There was a great tradition of
harness racing in that part of the country,
and my uncle began training horses
years before. Now the barns and the track
were run-down, the track itself covered
with weeds; the old hands, the trainers,
slept in ragged bunks in the sheds,
but worked the horses each day
in the dusty wake of their existence.

That day I had an idea.
I told my cousin to lead St. Mary
down the path that led to the
training track almost a mile away.
It took forever for us to plod down there.
She would hesitate, snort, and
try to turn, and I could feel the
tenseness in her neck as my cousin Ray
led her onto the track. Suddenly
she stomped and adjusted sideways.

It happened very quickly.
I remember the old mare lifting
her head, and sniffing the air, giving off
a sigh that seemed to come from something
deeper than a tired heart.
Before I knew it, St. Mary exploded:
she took off at full speed around
the track, me grabbing hold of her mane,
my face buried in her neck.
Her speed increased as we
made the first turn, and at that point
all the old trainers came running
out of their sheds, waving their arms
and shouting something at us.

It was no use.
Nothing could stop St. Mary. In her mind
she still had one lap to go.
Oddly, my own fright began to ease.
I was hanging on good and St. Mary
eased into her smooth pacing trot.
I was beginning to enjoy it.
She never let up until she crossed
the finish line.

The trainers and my uncle Arthur
caught up with us as the old champ

slowed to a halt. A foamy sweat encased
her—she was white with the heavy lather,
almost ghost-like, but her girth was
blowing in and out like a huge bellows.
They rubbed her, wiped her, walked her
and covered her with a blanket.
She could have died, I was told,
running that speed, and I
could have been thrown off as well.

I guess we lucked out that day,
St. Mary getting her last race, revisiting
a moment of glory. And me,
racing a great horse, leaving the world
behind for a moment while I rode
with a champion.
In the pasture, about a month later,
St. Mary perked up her head
when I walked over, and nuzzled my shoulder
gently, affectionately.
For her, for me now some sixty years later,
God rest her soul, we were giving
a little thanks to each other:
memories create companions.

Lady of Sorrow

SOMETIMES DETAILS SEEM TOO appropriate to be true. "Lady of Sorrow" is a perfect name for the church in Louise NiCastro's story. Of course she is the lady in sorrow, remembering a disappointment that still haunts her more than sixty years later. The metaphor too is appropriate—the voice that defines the lyrical, expressive character, silenced because of parents too strict to understand a basic need. I like this story because Louise, although from the old school, is not afraid to voice her old resentment of her parents' actions—though she acknowledges her love for them. These feelings, in fact, get worse over the years, the sorrow deepening. But there is, in the end, an irony: her story is the beautiful song she longs to sing. The "daughter of Michelina" elicits our praises once again. ■

Lady of Sorrow
Louise NiCastro

I WAS SITTING IN the pew
at Lady of Sorrow Church
on Niagara Street
one warm Sunday morning
when Father Moffet asked me
to fill in with the choir.

I remember, to my
astonishment, everyone turning around
after the first song,
and for a moment I thought
I had embarrassed myself.
But the faces were kind,
a few people nodding approvingly,
and even the organist
seemed very pleased.

After church, I heard
a few of the church-goers whispering,
"That is Michelina's daughter,"
and they praised my voice
and suddenly the world was different.
Father Moffet then came up,
taking time from greeting the
parishioners and asked me to join the
choir, permanently....

I was only eleven,
and those were the days
when parents made your decisions
and we were obedient always.
When it came to the evening
for rehearsal, my parents whispered
together,
and I was told that seven o'clock in the evening

was too late for a young girl to be out,
and that, as the saying goes, was that.

So there I sat every Sunday,
sitting there in Our Lady of Sorrow,
my own sorrow deepening
as I heard the choir singing,
and then, heard my own voice,
rising above the others in my mind,
a voice that would be missing
from that time on as the silence grew
in the cathedral of my own regret.

And to this day,
I feel even worse, thinking back
over the years, my voice
almost a mystery sometimes
as I sing in my anger, in my joy,
no one to hear, no voices
to blend with...
I still feel hurt over the lost chance to sing.

The Gift

ONE AFTERNOON AT ONE of our weekly sessions at
Kennedy Towers, we exchanged stories about
Christmases past. I remember Mamie Lee Haynes
explaining that her mother used to leave broken
pieces of glass in the fireplace, claiming Santa must
have broken the toys. It seemed like a variation of
the coal story, though even more sinister, and I
thought what might follow would be a condemna-
tion of her mother or those early years. One must
listen—be patient—when allowing a story to un-
fold. Once Mamie began recalling other details
from those Christmases past, the story was trans-
formed into one of love, hardship, and finally the
incredible initiation of mutual respect between
daughter and mother. "The Gift" became the text of
a Christmas card the City of Rochester printed and
passed out free to children and senior citizens.■

The Gift
Mamie Lee Haynes

WE KEPT WONDERING WHY he didn't come
every year.
And Ma would say, well, the yard's a mess
and Santa don't like no messy yard
to park his sleigh in.
So that year we swept the dirt yard,
cleaned the hen coop daily, crawled
under the house and pulled out the
garbage,
picked up the leaves, and even
painted the front gate with whitewash.
On Christmas morning we found pieces of
broken glass in our fireplace.
Ma said, well, I guess he broke his toys
when he landed, and left.
Turns out, though, we didn't find out
till years later, Ma broke up some old
crystal glass in the fireplace.

So that next year, we swept and cleaned
and picked up the yard even harder.
But my hopes were fading
being the oldest of our bunch (Ma would
have thirteen of us in all!)
so I started gathering some sticks and
tall grasses, and some material my ma
and her friends who sewed for the white folk
had around.
I tied the grass together, making a ball of it
for the head, rolling the hair, and covering
the dolls with beautiful dresses of
gingham, pongee, or linen or whatever I
could get ahold of and sew together.
And that Christmas
I had a doll for every one of

my brothers and sisters.
But when I got up early to put them
out by the fireplace that morning, expecting
nothing but maybe some pieces of broken
glass,
I saw the most beautiful basket of apples,
oranges and nuts I had ever seen.
My ma looked at me
and I looked at her
while my brothers and sisters held their
dolls
and touched the fruit in the basket.
I was only ten or so
but I understood, and so did she,
the gift we had together:
Santa had come to our house.

The Orchard Photograph

ONCE IN AWHILE, TRYING to garner new subject matter for our stories, I ask people to bring in old photographs and to tell the story of one photo. Mary Wagner brought in a photo of some young people posing in a field in front of a blossoming cherry tree. We were taken by the beauty of Dolores in the photo—and before long Mary's story reminded us again of the depth and resonance of such beauty. Mary's recollection brought the photo to life. That's what literature does—it brings photos, wherever they exist, to life. ■

The Orchard Photograph

Mary Wagner

IT'S SPRING.
The perfumed blossoms
Held a flush of pink at their
white centers, as if
a velvet cheek, a sudden blush,
could be seen showing through.

We were together that day,
sitting in the tall, yellowish grass
of the orchard.
I don't remember who took the photo,
but we posed
in the warm May sun,
my cousins, sisters, and me,
glad to be together.
I remember Dolores most that day,
her laughter catching the early wind
of the season,
so lovely in her tailored red dress,
so in love with her young sailor, Harold,
who'd disappear some time later,
lost overseas along with some
of the joy Dolores would never regain.

To visit the country,
my sisters and I chose floral dresses;
we wanted to blend with the flowing
meadows
on the outskirts of Sodus.
Under the blue sky, we took off our shoes
and walked through the dry grass
holding hands in a circle around Frances,
my sister,
who was sixteen that day
and blushing, like the pink

at the center of the cherry blossom,
when we sang out a rhyme
about a girl's first kiss.

Too soon we hear
my aunt's voice; the birthday cake
is ready, lit by
the candles of a teenager's joy.
But it was Dolores,
more radiant than any flame,
whose eyes filled with the sparkle
of our own romantic notions,
mentioning her sailor so often
we felt his presence, too,
a shadow lengthening in late afternoon.
So we left the orchard,
the serenity of a moment so brief,
and yet
captured forever, now, by a simple
photograph.

I think of Dolores, her love defined
by the years of misery and grief.
And when I do
I feel the warmth of that Spring day
the perfumed blossoms, the flush
of pink at their white centers,
as if a velvet cheek, a sudden blush
could be seen showing through.

Knowing Where, How, and Ourselves

IF WE ARE TO pass anything to our children, it must be how, in our own young days, we worked to survive. I remember the self-assured, wise look in Sarah McClellan's eyes as she uttered the opening sentence of this poem—"There's an advantage to being a country girl." She knew it—and by the end of her story, we knew it too. This poem describes how she did a chore as a young girl some seventy years ago, riding mules to a gristmill. It's a story about work and the importance of knowing who we are by what we are able to do for ourselves. It is a story, I must admit, that makes me feel a bit inadequate. Perhaps if we allow ourselves to feel inadequate enough, we'll take a closer look at the world around us, realizing again the relationship between what we do and who we are. ■

Knowing Where, How, and Ourselves
Sarah McClellan

THERE'S AN ADVANTAGE TO being a country girl . . .

I ducked my head riding Old Blue,
one of the two mules we owned,
when we passed under those big old
oaks along the dirt road,
cause here and there snakes would be
hanging from the limbs, long and black,
wound around the branches.
And even the sweet scent of the pines
couldn't erase my fear, there
in the hills of Mississippi in the
fresh warmth of the morning
when I'd bring the corn to the gristmill.

I was twelve, I reckon,
and I'd spent the night before
shelling the corn with Ma
till our hands were raw, piling up the cobs
behind the stove for burnwood.
No, we didn't throw anything away,
found a need for everything.
So in the morning, after making grits
and biscuits and syrup,
and cooking up some meat from one
of our butchered hogs;
after getting Pa and the boys
out in the field to pick cotton and tobacco,
Ma and I dragged the corn sacks
on top of either Old Blue or Kate,
heaving those sacks over the back end
of one of those mules,
and I'd make my way to the mill.

Mr DeLong was a kindly old gentleman,
a tall white man with a wrinkled face.
He'd always greet me with a smile, and
help me off that big old mule,
and take the sacks of corn for me too.
After it was ground, he'd
take his toll bucket and fill it,
taking his fair share of corn meal,
and before he'd help me back onto the mule,
he'd fix the sacks on either side
of Kate or Old Blue, and he'd throw the
sack of husks over the mules' backs too,
which I'd bring back for the chickens and hogs.

On the way home, I'd duck again
under those old oak trees, hoping
I wouldn't come across a snake hanging so.
So I held close to the neck of that mule
while the white womanfolk rode
their horses by, sitting erect so
with the slit up the side of their
riding dresses...as if no snake would
dare touch them.
And when I got back I'd have
no time to think about much except
that more biscuits had to be made
and the meat cooked, and the sidewalk
swept for my pa and brothers coming
back from the fields.

It was tough work, thinking back,
but that was the life
of a country girl, the advantage really.
Cause we knew, I mean *knew*
what we ate, knew it from the ground
that it came from. And we knew
what we wore, from the cotton in our hands
to the corn sack made into a party dress.

Yes, we knew where everything we needed
came from. It was our world around us,
and the hard work was simply
the respect we gave to our daily bread.

The New Shoes

A MONTH AFTER "THE New Shoes" appeared in the Gannett newspapers in Rochester, Rose Muscarella died. Her story concludes with a dream of her meeting her mother on the spiral staircase of their hotel and walking off together to eternity. And that's how I'm sure many who knew Rose envisioned her after her death—such is the power and magic of literature. As a matter of fact her family invited me to read this poem as a kind of eulogy at her funeral mass, which I did. This section of this book is about initiations into strange, often difficult moments which change our lives. What I have noticed in the eyes of many, including those of Rose, is an endearing, enduring love that grew out of encounters that left us with psychological wounds. It is the wound from which art—that affirmation of life which affords us our brief celebrations—springs forth. To use Rose's beautiful metaphor, we scrub the marble steps until we are tired, and then we make our elegant departure. ∎

The New Shoes

Rose Muscarella

FUNNY HOW A LIFE
can change because you need
a pair of shoes...

It was in the winter of 1921.
I was twelve.
My father died, just like that,
leaving eight of us and my mother
with not much except
our love for each other.

I remember how they lined us up
there in an enormous room
at Catholic Charities, where we went
for shoes that snowy day.
I was the oldest, and they
lined us up by height, all the way
down to my eight-month-old baby sister
in the arms of my mama.
One by one, baby first,
they brought us shoes, black patent leather
shoes, slippers for the babies,
hightops for the rest of us.
One of my younger sisters
asked if it was Christmas, and it just
as well might have been that year.

They gave my mom something too....
A job. They arranged for her
to wash floors for a hotel downtown.
Now I had been in a "dunce" class,
as we called it, at school,
learning how to cook and make clothes
and take care of the house.
And suddenly, at twelve years old,

that's what I was doing,
quitting school and taking care
of the family.

One day I wrapped several
of my younger brothers and sisters
with warm clothes, and pushed
the baby carriage a long, long way,
all the way down South Avenue,
to see the hotel
where my mama worked.
The babies were cold and tired
and I tried to quiet them down some
when we entered the lobby.

We must have looked strange
there amidst the grand splendor of
the Hotel Bristol, holding hands
and gathered around the baby carriage,
dwarfed by the stately columns
and polished wood trimmings,
while the suited bellboys
and white-tied managers
looked us over and spoke with
their hands held close to their mouths.
Then we looked over to the left
and saw what we came to see.

There was Mama
in her blue workdress, sitting
halfway up the most elegant spiral,
white marble staircase anyone
could imagine.
She was scrubbing the stairs with
a rag, a bucket by her side.
When she saw us, she waved,
looking so tired and beautiful
on that spiral stairway.

I remember feeling hurt that afternoon,
seeing her on her hands and knees
washing the marble steps.
The elegance of the staircase only
emphasized the poor,
insignificant figure upon it.

We made our way home that day,
a little exhausted by our trip.
I got supper ready,
and Mama came home as happy as ever.
All of us were so close, like a
stairway really, each year a step
between us, each step a journey
we all shared.

I'm eighty-four years old now,
and my steps are cautious
and deliberate, steadied often
by a cane.
I walk painfully up stairs, but
when I do I imagine
I'm on that spiral staircase
in the lobby of the Bristol Hotel.
I keep imagining how elegant
the rooms must be at the top of the stairs.

And when I reach the last marble stair,
it is my mother I discover
scrubbing the final step, looking at me
and dropping the rag into the bucket,
rising to her feet and
holding out her arm, which I take
in mine; and together we walk
down the steps, our new shoes gleaming,
making our way home.

Possessions

The Cooling Board

I THOUGHT MATTIE WHITLEY had told "her story" in the emotionally charged *Train Ride*. But it seems she had another powerful story lodged even deeper in her memory. It began simply enough with a conversation in our group about unexpected deaths there in the rural South back in the Twenties. I did not know the term "cooling board," but everyone else there knew it, and soon it was made vivid in my mind. It seemed almost by chance that Mattie offered the details of her mother's death from the Spanish Flu, and though her description of it seemed interesting enough to be recorded, the bombshell was, of course, the story of her father's quick exit hidden in a casket to Ohio. Mattie was very reluctant to elaborate on the experience, telling us that this was something she had never told *anyone* else. Well, she told us, recollecting the details as we pressed in our bewilderment for more information; and the more she revealed about this brief, tragic time in her life, the more we seemed to find in ourselves the depth of understanding that seemed equally well-hidden. Of course that's the power of these personal histories—the more one reaches out, the more we all reach in. And what we discover, as Mattie recalls in her story, is not encumbered by the "howls of bloodhounds in the night," but nurtured with "the heartbeat of enduring love." ■

The Cooling Board
Mattie Whitley

NO ONE WANTED
to shroud* the young ones,
the babies that died
just a few days old,
but I did once, a little cousin
during that time after World War One
when the flu from Spain struck
and people everywhere got weak
and feverish, and sick to their stomachs.
So many died down there
in Georgia, they finally
disallowed funerals altogether,
burying people immediately,
and it was then, I remember,
when the churches began filling
everyday, and it was at the church
where we held together
what we had.

So we were used to the dying,
my sisters and brothers
and me,
though I was only nine.
But when it was my mama
suddenly on the cooling board,
her life gone after just
a few days of fever, it was not
something we could understand.
And as she lay there
on the wood planks that lay on top of
two cane bottom chairs,
some neighbor women rubbed
her body clean with cotton cloths,

*shroud: covering a dead body with a white cloth

then covered her with a white sheet,
put the saucer of salt
on her chest,
placed buffalo nickels on her eyes,
and we all kept the cats
out of the house.
And after a day or two
my daddy pulled some planks
off one of the old cotton houses
and made a casket
that we buried her in.
In Forsythe Georgia, in 1922,
on a small farm
with six kids and no mama,
life goes on,
and we hardly got used
to doing all the new chores
when one night
while my daddy slept with the babies
we heard the bloodhounds barking
and one of my daddy's friends
ran into the house
and I remember everyone crying
and my oldest brother
quiet and scared and knowing
a little more than the rest of us.
And Daddy dressed real quick
and told us he had to
leave right away,
and that would be the last
we'd see of him for a long, long time.

It turned out my daddy
a couple days earlier
went down to check the corn
he'd planted by the river,
because there'd been heavy rains
and it might have been

too wet to cultivate.
He came upon the Gold Dust vendor,
the one-horse wagon
with the canvas top,
ransacked, most of the soap powder,
tobacco, snuff and cracker jacks
already gone.
And the vendor, my daddy discovered,
beat-up and unconscious.
Now in those days
a black man found next to an unconscious
white man was a dead man.
And my daddy ran fast and far away
from all that.
Once the word got out,
the white moonshiners from across
the river, who wanted
my daddy's moonshine business all along,
blamed him.

Of course the Masonics stepped in,
knowing my daddy was innocent,
selling his buggy, mule,
and milk cow,
saving him that night from a lynching,
and arranging for him
to travel in a casket, like a dead man,
on a train from Georgia
to Cleveland, Ohio.
I couldn't help but think of
my mama in her casket, dreaming
that long peaceful sleep,
and my daddy in his casket,
scared for his life,
dreaming too
of a new life, if he made it,
in the north with no wife,
no family, no farm.

My father's sister
took me and Mary Ola, my sister.
Another relative took two of my brothers
and another sister,
and still another relative
took the baby and we pretty much
didn't see each other any more.
My sister and I
passed onto another of
my father's sisters, then onto
my grandmother,
and all the while we could not understand
how we lost our entire family
so quickly that year.

We saw Daddy again
ten years later, in 1932
in East Point, Georgia, where
both Mary Ola and me got married.
I can still see him picking up
my son James, just over a year old,
his grandson, into his arms
and smiling that smile
we had seen so many times
so many years before.
And it seemed so natural, so right,
I remember,
a man stepping out of his casket,
stepping out of his grief
and out of his years on the run,
and holding a grandson
up to the light of the sky
that echoed no longer with the howl
of bloodhounds in the night,
but with the heartbeat of enduring love.

Three Brothers

CORNELIA PHELPS DOESN'T TALK much. She gets a look on her face though, a wise little smirk that lets you know there's something in the heart. You have to look for these things when you interview story-tellers, especially the reluctant ones. Once we got the names of her brothers, and found out that they all had died years earlier, we asked all kinds of questions about them. As any writer would, I zeroed in on one specific detail about each brother, and those details lent themselves very naturally to their metaphoric composition. The result is a short poetic tribute to each brother, as well as the perfect reflection of Cornelia's humble, loving character. ■

Three Brothers
Cornelia Phelps

1. Tump

TUMP DIED EARLY,
when I was just a teenager.
An epileptic fit,
that shaking that shakes me still
when I think of the brother
I knew so briefly and
loved so much.
I can still see him working
on a truck, under the hood,
moving his hands so swiftly,
knowing just what to do.
He'd make anything run smooth
but he couldn't
steady himself that day
when his body shook the life
right out of him,
and there was nothing that could
stop him from leaving us.

II. Tommy

He loved his baby sister
and he would do
anything for me.
He'd take a nickel out of his pocket
and my eyes would sparkle
all the way
to the country store,
where I'd buy myself
some peanut candy, and finish it
before I got back home.
His heart was just too big,
I reckon,

and that's how he died, a heart
too great for the chest of a man.

III. Lewis

He drove a crane
and broke up houses with it,
getting a kick out of
all that destruction.
But when he got home
and started with me, cause we
fought all the time,
he always got the worst of it,
and I'd hang onto him
as he tried to scamper out
the door, probably wishing
he'd stayed in his crane all night,
threatening the moon
instead of me.
But I loved him, and when
they discovered that spot on his lung,
it was like someone started
tearing a house down,
and finally he too collapsed altogether.

In Gainville, Georgia

As I SAID, CORNELIA Phelps doesn't say much. But she did tell us of an incident in the town where she grew up, the killing of a black man and the dragging of his body through the streets—and she compared the brutal affair to the stomping and beating of Rodney King by police in Los Angeles in 1991, which we witnessed time and time again on our television screens. Apparently many people like Cornelia replay over and over in their minds the violent injustices witnessed over the years. Here was a chance to express once more, "in writing" and in poetic outrage, the indignity felt for so many years. And in the end, once again, in the Black American folk tradition, nature takes the place of the law and restores a sense of justice to those who, for too long a time in this country, had no way to defend their rights or themselves. ■

In Gainville, Georgia

Cornelia Phelps

WHITE FOLK BEAT UP
the poor soul,
beat him dead—and no one
really knew why, but by then
it didn't matter much
as they dragged his body
through the streets of Gainville.

We know the history
of it all—so we don't blink
when we see a black man
being kicked and beaten one night
in L.A. by a bunch of policemen.
In Bishop, I heard my mama
talk about a colored man
tied to a pole, soaked with kerosene
and set to flame....

But we go on,
knowing justice takes its own road,
sometimes the long, twisting
dirt backroads so long forgotten
in America.
And in the end
we arrive at the same destination,
though some of us
are tired and old.

In Gainville, a few days
later, a hurricane
swept the neighborhood of
those white folk.
In Bishop, each one
who struck a match that day

died of a heart attack
less than a year later.

Everyone gets what's coming.

Marvin

SOMETIMES THE WORDS OF loved ones stay with a person a long time. The words of Rosie Mitchell's nephew—"In ten days I'm leaving here"—begin her story just as they began her recollection that day in our Monday morning workshop at the North Street Community Center. I'm always amazed at how naturally metaphor creates itself — how it becomes the focus of a story even to those who have no idea of the meaning of the term. Rosie understood, in the midst of her rendering, that she too one day would ride that train, not simply the train of death, but the journey to reunification and joy. No wonder Rosie, despite her hard life, seems content and happy. ■

Marvin

Rosie Mitchell

"IN TEN DAYS I'M leaving here."
I looked at my nephew
there in the hospital bed, so weak
from the pneumonia, the i.v.'s
in his thin arms,
the cancer eating away at him.

He told me he could manage
when I doubted him.
Marvin always did things for himself.
I know, because
I helped raise him from one year up.
He was forty-two,
and his pride grew with the years.

"I'm going to ride the train,"
he said, for a moment looking for
a pack of cigarettes to
take along. I asked him
where he was going.
"I don't know," he answered,
"but I'm going to leave this place."

Nine days later he was gone—
one day earlier than
he'd planned. He was always
a little anxious to get things done.
I know I'll meet him one day,
there, waiting on the platform
of the train station.

I guess I'll step on that train
and he'll be there,
sitting near the window, looking out
at that view along the countryside,

smoking a cigarette
and smiling at me as I
throw my suitcase back on the platform,
through with that luggage forever.

I'll take a seat next to him,
anxious for the next stop,
knowing my mother will be there,
my brother, and even my grandmother.
I'll wait for the porter
to call out the destinations,
that song of joy that takes us away.

The State Troopers

ROSE MUSCARELLA, LIKE MANY of the storytellers in this collection, never even got close to making it through public school. As I recall, Rose quit school (see her earlier story, "The New Shoes") at about age twelve. But this story is a social portrait of a time when racial hatred was rampant in the streets of America. In the sixties there was a major riot in Rochester, New York and since I grew up in the midst of it I remember it well. Rose's story, quite beautifully, catches the nuances of the complicated human relationships in the neighborhoods—the troopers on the lawn chairs, the husband brandishing his shotgun, and of course Tillie, the black neighbor playing the piano and singing for everyone there in the midst of all that violence and hatred. It is a vivid moment, an insightful rendering of a country too confused to see itself or heal itself. ■

The State Troopers
Rose Muscarella

THEY SAT IN THE lawn chairs
we set up for them
in our backyard.
There was a loveseat swing
with wrought iron arms
and Italian flowers pressed
into the metal seat.
They seemed to enjoy it.

Once in a while
we heard a gunshot echo
through the neighborhood.
One of the troopers
would shake his head, put on
his hat, and walk down the driveway
and look up and down the street.
Later, we moved the coffee pot
to the front porch.
Some of the neighbors would stop over;
perhaps because of the troopers
being there.

But my husband Joe got out
his shotgun anyway,
and stood on the front steps,
like a soldier from another time,
another place.
One of the troopers, with his hand
on Joe's shoulder,
talked him into putting the gun
back in the attic.
I made some lemonade against the
intermittent sirens of the streets.

Even the black family next door
came over to stay with us.
They seemed more afraid than we were.
Tillie was an entertainer,
playing the piano for the rich
in another part of the city.
She played for us one night; the troopers
gathered around our piano,
clapping their hands and singing
with their huge voices.
We all laughed so hard we forgot
about the looting
and the shooting, and the bad feelings
and calloused hands gripping rocks
and sticks
during the racial riots of 1964.

Look Ma, No Hands:
A Cop's Memory of an Early Scam

HOW PREVAILING IS THE influence of literature? Gordon Urlacher, who told this story of an incident from his childhood, is the former police chief of Rochester who was prosecuted and convicted by the federal government of embezzlement and fraud. During his trial, the prosecuting attorney used this story in order to "prove" to the jury that the former police chief had been a liar early in his life! I don't think this had any effect, thank goodness, on the trial itself, but I do think that Gordon Urlacher's story illustrates beautifully the universal difficulties that exist in the relationship between a father and a teenage son. ■

Look, Ma, No Hands:
A Cop's Memories of an Early Scam
Gordon Urlacher

NOW I WAS A pretty good kid. And at thirteen I already had the inclination of a true American: to be mobile and thrifty.

It was the last day of classes at St. Ambrose, with exams starting the next day. I guess my friend John and I wanted to get a quick adventuresome jump into summer; at least we figured, it being such a beautiful day, we'd get a nice, quick easy ride home. We hopped a Rochester City Transit bus down Clifford Avenue.

I don't think we made a block and a half.

We were on the corner of Culver and Clifford when we jumped on. We held onto a cardboard sign attached to the bus. We were fine for about fifty to sixty feet, but when the bus began to pick up speed and we noticed there was no place for our feet, John said, "We're gonna fall."

Dangling there, I remember saying "Don't worry," just as the cardboard sign gave way. We must have tumbled a good distance.

I remember two things that struck me as I rolled and skidded to a rest in the middle of Clifford Avenue. First, my arms hurt. Second, John seemed to have done a double somersault as he fell, actually landing on his feet, as if purposely doing a gymnastic stunt. I think it was then the notion came to me that there were two kinds of people in the world: one blessed with grace, sporting a physical accommodation with the world whatever the difficulty; and the other—to which I know I belonged—who would find in their agony a remarkable ability to tolerate pain.

By this time, I knew at least one of my arms was broken.

Between the wrath of our parents and that of the bus company, John went on to convince me, we were in trouble—no way, he reasoned, could we tell anyone how it happened. I agreed, of course, minute by minute more concerned about the growing pain and stiffness in my arms.

The strategy came to us simply, almost splendidly, like a grand notion. An untimely, unfortunate, adolescently innocent fall off a bike!

We made our way to a friend's house on Edgeland Drive, a couple of blocks away—a kid named Sal. We told him what happened, borrowed his bicycle and made our way back to Clifford Avenue, looking for the highest curb we could find. After we picked the spot we went back to Sal's and called my parents.

When they showed up at the high curb and the discarded bike at the corner of Edgeland and Clifford a few minutes later, they were so concerned, so anxious to get me to a hospital, there really wasn't much attention paid to how it happened. It was, in their unsuspecting minds, a bike accident—no one ever questioning it. I remember thinking how small a part truth played in the presence of sympathy.

At the hospital, the doctors put on one cast and sent me home. A few hours later, my other arm was hurting so, my parents took me back and the doctors discovered that arm was broken, too. They put on another cast, only this time a half cast so I could bend my arm a little—"You don't want to do everything for him," the doctor laughed, winking at my parents, "especially in the bathroom—you know what I mean...."

I didn't feel like laughing myself, but I'm sure everyone was relieved that I could bend at least one of my arms a little.

And so, for a couple of months, my life changed a bit. I'd like to think that everything adds to character—and that a little physical indisposition makes one reflective, more contemplative. I mean, look what it did for my academic stature at St. Ambrose that year.

I had dreaded the English exam in Sister Florence's class. But the first good news lifted my spirits: I would receive the full forty credits for the writing section of the exam—since, with both arms in casts I could barely hold a pencil, let alone write with one. The rest of the exam was multiple choice.

And that, given the nature of nuns to grimace at the thought of marking down a wrong answer on anyone's behalf, turned out to be a great advantage. When I gave a wrong answer, there was always such a painful hesitation I knew from that involuntary reflex to change it, which I did often.

The right answers, however, were met with a pleasant sigh. The lowest mark I received on any exam that year, eighth grade at Saint Ambrose, was 92! I guess a lot of people assumed I did well under pressure.

Two nights after the "accident" I made my parents help me put on the Pony League baseball uniform and take me to the game. I sat there on the bench, both casts already half-filled with signatures, shouting encouragements to my teammates.

Some things just disappeared that summer: pitching, the newspaper route, bikes, girls....

But, in my dependency on a few maneuverable hands around the house, I did get closer to my parents—especially my dad. There was one daily routine that seems to represent the awkwardness, disgust, care and ultimate love between a son and a father.

Now before I broke my arms I took great care combing my hair. There was a certain style that I knew was the real Gordie Urlacher—sort of back on the sides into a moderate d.a., and the front kind of falling forward in a casual curl or two down my forehead. What I would call more or less a boy's Italian Ricky Nelson. My father hated it.

But to satisfy me, he took great pains every day to comb my hair the way I liked it. Unfortunately, those were the days of Vitalis and the "wet look." The problem was that my father, being of another generation and another hairstyle to boot, could not get used to hair going anywhere except flat against the skull in some orderly direction. So every time a piece of hair sprang up instinctively toward the curls I was cultivating he'd attack it with a hand full of Vitalis. I could only watch.

The irony was, of course, that although he hated my hairstyle, he was trying desperately to comb it the way I liked it.

At the same time I hated the feel of all that grease, and the more my father tried to please me, the more gook he'd plaster on. I remember looking into the mirror, my casts heavy on my arms, my hair looking abnormally wet, and feeling absolutely helpless.

Perhaps it was simply adolescence, now that I look back.

Except for understanding I'd never hop a bus again, I didn't know much.

I didn't like living with the guilt of the lie I told (I'd tell everyone four years later in a humorous essay I wrote for an English class at East High—no more multiple choices!), and it sure wasn't any fun looking on from the bench at the ballpark at Norton Village.

But then again John said we had a secret, and I guess we did. And Sister Mary Timothy said these things build character, and I guess they do.

And it could give me another story to tell somewhere down the road—like tonight, this memory a mirror in which I catch young Gordie, whatever his troubles, flashing a little grin.

Hands: A Love Poem

I OFTEN USE THIS poem in my workshop on writing
love poetry. Rose Venturelli's story was so imme-
diately compelling, the intensity of her recollection
so clear in the contrasting emotions of love and
disappointment. Oddly, when I read it now, it
seems as if I never wrote it, that I simply recorded
the details she was anxious to share with our
group until the ending, the emotional climax, just
appeared, like a sigh at the end of a story. The
mind chooses its details, like a camera magically
clicking on its own as it scans one's personal histo-
ries—and the final portrait appears, like some
ancient Polaroid negative held to the light for half
a century until the images become clear. ■

Hands: A Love Poem
Rose Venturelli

MY HUSBAND CUT HIS hand
in a machine that he thought
he could run in the shop
where he worked, bad enough—parts
of a thumb and a finger cut right off—
so he'd remember forever.

I remember that summer day
in 1923, waiting for him
to come home from the hospital,
standing by the window
looking out at Central Park,
the grass so green and trimmed
along the island between the streets,
the maple trees fluttering their big leaves
in the occasional breeze,
and in the yards of my neighbors
the lilacs opening in a blue and violet
welcoming of summer.
I married Vincent (we called him Jimmy)
two years earlier
and we were happy in those first years,
putting our house together
and Jimmy working hard so we could have
the best of Sunday dinners.
And we'd have three children before long,
two boys and a girl to steady our love
and help carry me through the days,
the years Jimmy's mind
started playing tricks on him,
taking him away from us so often, so long,
more than fifty years in the Veterans Hospital
in Canandaigua....

But that day, when I saw the Dago flyer,
the Central Park trolley
filled with Italians like us with, as the
joke went, garlic on their breath—
when I saw the trolley
I quickly made the bed, because
Jimmy liked the house neat
and here he was coming home without
part of his hand,
and I rushed trying to please him so.

And when I finished
I happened to look at my hand —
my wedding ring was gone,
just a bare knuckle where the
one-carat diamond had been.

We looked all afternoon,
and that night my father came over
and we pulled the bedroom apart
looking for the ring,
but no one found it....
It just vanished.

And it never was found;
I remember missing it so,
maybe not the same way as Jimmy missed
the ends of his finger and thumb,
but I remember some fifty years later sitting
at Jimmy's bedside at the VA hospital
as my poor lost husband lay dying....

I remember holding his hand
that last afternoon of his life,
and seeing his fingers that had been
cut off so early in his days,
and seeing my own finger so bare
where the ring had never been replaced,

and seeing our hands together,
and knowing whatever was missing,
the diamond, the flesh,
had been replaced with care and love.

We held tight,
each heart giving a final squeeze,
and then we let go
and all the pain and sorrow
fell away from our hands
until nothing seemed to be missing any more.

Seclusions

Coming to America

I HAD HEARD STORIES similar to Rose Venturelli's "Coming To America." My grandfather (Rosario, after whom I'm named), in fact, came to America by himself in similar circumstances, sending for his family some time after he arrived. But Rose's story was compelling—she was incredibly anxious to tell it, interrupting others in our group until it was the focus of our dialogue. I remember especially the moment she uttered the line that "America had everything except a father for me." That statement reflected not only the core of this particular story, but, hauntingly, also reflected a universal condition—the sad trade-offs we make when we leave a tradition for a "better life." What I like about Rose's story too is that she gives us a vivid glimpse of both moments, leaving Italy and arriving in America. It must have been a terrifying time for many of our ancestors, and we must remind ourselves now and then what others had to go through for what was our ultimate benefit. ∎

Coming to America
Rose Venturelli

I DON'T REMEMBER MUCH in Mondo Oro,
the Sicilian village where I was born
just at the turn of the century.
I remember the day the village
opened the coffin of a priest
who had been buried a long time;
if he'd been well preserved,
they would have anointed him a saint.

I remember too
carrying a white towel
to assist in the baptism of a baby.

And I remember people yelling angrily
in the midst of the somber
of my grandfather's funeral, when a
distant relative was caught
trying to steal the wax from the candles...

No, I don't remember much
from my half-dozen years as a child
in Sicily, except that my father
left when I was three,
went to America to work in a coal mine
in Pennsylvania, and left us behind.

I guess he had enough
when my mother's third child
died at birth, and when his ninth horse
died as well. He had a dream
of a better life, and he went off
to America.

I remember getting into
the horse-drawn wagon the day we left

for the boat that would take us
to America and my father.

I was probably six years old, and
my mother gave me a very small bag
to pack, so I left all my toys
to my best friend, and she promised
to keep them for me.

On our way to the port
my grandmother stopped us,
and I remember how she cried
and begged us not to go to America,
because she felt that assured her
of never seeing her son, my father, again.
I put my hands over my ears,
and closed my eyes,
and imagined the sea as pure a blue
as the Sicilian sky above us.

At the port, for luck, some of us
threw coins from the boat, and
I can still see the young boys
we left behind, tearing off their shirts
and diving into the water
to retrieve the coins.

But no one felt too lucky
once we put to sea, so many of us
huddled-up in the open bunks
on the lower deck,
and on the rough days, with the
boat rolling one way then another,
my mom gathered a bunch of pans
and had me run from one sick person
to another to catch the throw-up.
I don't know how many days
we spent at sea,

but we were very relieved
to see the port at New York,
our first glimpse of America.

To begin with, someone put us
on the wrong train, heading north
instead of south to Pennsylvania.
When my mother tried to tell
someone, she stated her most basic predicament:
"No capisce Englise." And everyone
thought she was hungry and
brought her food!

Finally, after so much confusion,
and my mother convinced by others to
enter a taxi whose driver
she did not trust,
she drove from the train station
to a small town in Pennsylvania
to the boarding house
which would be our new home.
Two men stood in the doorway,
and when my mother told me
to greet my father
I ran to the arms of the wrong man.

No, I don't remember much
except that one night an uncle
came by and explained my father
had to work overtime
and asked if he could get some
of his clothes.
I guess no one wanted to tell us
what happened, how my father
died that day in a coal mine accident,
and the clothes had been requested
by the undertaker.

I remember how they
opened my father's eyes in the coffin
so someone could take a photograph.
I remember how it seemed
I had closed my eyes so slightly,
nothing more than a blink perhaps,
and our lives changed
and how America had everything
except a father for me.

My mother sold just about everything
to pay people back for
the $75 they contributed
for the funeral, including the
velvet coat I loved dearly.
We stayed in the boarding house
for a couple of weeks,
but we had no money for rent.
I remember wishing I had some
of the toys I'd left behind,
and how I'd see my grandmother's face as
she pleaded with us not to go to America.

Someone said they knew people
up north where we could stay,
and the next day
we were on a train heading for Buffalo.

Doing the Wash in Bainbridge, 1925

MAMIE HAYNES PUT HER hands nervously to her face when she revealed the "crime" of the Homers, the white family she worked for back in the '30s in Georgia. This was a story she kept to herself for almost fifty years. The thought of it still frightened her. We hear about the brutal encounters blacks experienced in the South, but it isn't often we are given a first-hand account by an eyewitness. I can imagine a young Miss Haynes in 1935 trying to get through the day until she could make her way out of the door, never to return to the Homer place. It is interesting to note that the thought of "reporting a crime" never would occur to a black woman in those circumstances at that time and place. Genuine fear was the proper response, as was her flight the next day to Tallahassee. It is interesting to note also the end of Mamie's story, a common theme among black folk tales and recollections: nature comes back to take revenge on those who've committed crimes against others—in this case a storm that tore up Bainbridge. It represents, of course, the force of justice when there is no civil appeal possible. ■

Doing the Wash in Bainbridge, 1935
Mamie Haynes

"DON'T GET UP THE clothes,"
said Mrs. Homer, which seemed
odd to me.
I was cooking on the Homer range,
filling in for my sister
near Christmas time.

I was best at making
cornbread and sunfish, my
favorite dish, but I usually
got up the clothes too
from down in the laundry.
No one ever told me
not to get up the clothes.

It was 1935, in
Bainbridge, Georgia.
I was eighteen,
and there was trouble in the air,
just about everywhere.
Guidance, the colored boy
who drove that taxi cab,
asked for the hose to wash out
the inside of his car.
"Don't tell anybody," he whispered
to me, "but they killed Meaty McClyde."

Meaty had been accused
of killing a white woman and
her daughter, the woman being a friend
of the Homers', and the daughter
a girlfriend of Homer's son.

Whites took justice in
their own hands, and though Meaty

and others claimed his innocence,
they killed him that night.

They first cut off his privates
and stuck them in his mouth,
and drove him around
for people to see.
Then they cut him up
and laid parts of him
on porches of colored folk
and at the door of the doctor's office
and in the church.
Then they burned what was left
of him in the park
next to the colored school.

...But I went down
because it was my job
to get up the wash.
And that's where I found
Mr. Homer and his son's white shirt
all covered with blood.
Their pants looked like they was
dipped in blood.
Guidance came downstairs
and balled up all those clothes
and took them out and burned them.

I finished cooking the sunfish,
I don't know how,
and I told them politely
I was leaving.

But I didn't say I was
never coming back!
And I never did come back,
matter of fact, left
the next day for Tallahassee for good!

But I heard Meaty McClyde's mom
came up from Alabama
when she heard the news.
She went to church and wailed
about her son's innocence,
and that very day,
God's word,
a storm came up out of nowhere,
rain, lightning and thunder,
wind so strong it blew up the roots of trees in
Bainbridge.

When the Produce Warehouse Burned Down

JOHN TAYLOR'S REMINISCENCE IS simple and straightforward. This big, tough man with the gentle voice sat among us with a peaceful look on his face, remembering back to simpler, poorer times when he enjoyed life as a kid in rural Florida. I get the feeling, even now, that John felt a sense of belonging then, and that he could see that comfort disappear over the years. His choice of the burning of the produce market as a touchstone for the impending change is an apt one—the cheap produce represented both a means of making a living by harvesting crops and a means for survival even in the midst of poverty. ■

When the Produce Warehouse Burned Down

John Taylor

I REMEMBER THE NIGHT
we listened to the battery radio
in the light of the kerosene lamp,
Joe Louis beating Jim Braddock
for the world championship.
I guess it was hard times
for our parents,
though my father worked hard
hauling produce in a truck
and my mother took in clothes.

But we didn't know it,
friends and family gathered
on the porch,
me a happy ten-year-old
playing stickball,
hide-and-seek, and loving
our rented house.
Back then we didn't get
in much trouble.

But once we was arrested
for loitering ...where?
On our front porch!
And I remember
the handsome black soldier
arrested for eating in the restaurant
there in Jacksonville.

No, we'd stay on our own,
walking together three miles or so
to the movies, six cents
for three features and a serial.
In big crowds, the beach

or the circus, we'd hold on
to each other, afraid we'd get lost.

What changed?
I don't rightly know.
But I remember the day
the produce warehouse burned down
right to the ground.
From then on, there was no more
cheap produce, and they never
did rebuild it, and I knew life would
always be a little tougher from then on.

The Visit

SARAH HARMON IS QUITE a character, and in her story "The Visit" we can see her humor, her toughness, and her belief in the supernatural. There was no doubt among us that, indeed, she did see her parents by her bedside, long after they had died. Sarah recollects an experience shared in one form or another by a member of black women in our group—the husband who goes "exploring" eventually abandoning the household. Interestingly, Otis overhears Sarah talking in her sleep to her parents and accuses her of talking to another man; Sarah added with insight that he was "always saying how he'd wish he'd find one thing I did wrong so he wouldn't feel so bad about the way he treated me." The pipe incident reminds us of the volatile nature of the relationship, and we all had the relief of a laugh when Sarah asked God for the strength "to whip this man's behind." In the end, though, despite the anger, it is the disappointment she registers, noting again that she was expecting a lifetime of romance—but adding, with her knowing smile, she didn't figure on "only ten years." ■

The Visit

Sarah Harmon

I DON'T KNOW IF it was
a dream or not,
but there was my mama and papa
standing by my bedside
in the middle of the night
telling me to leave
that no-good husband lying next to me,
because if I didn't
something awful was gonna happen.

Now they had died
some years past, when I was just
in my teens, but they looked
like themselves standing there,
my mama in a light blue
house dress, and my daddy
in his bibbed farmer overalls.
They told me in the calmest voices
that Otis was planning
to kill me.
I had been praying to God
to show me a way out of that mess,
Otis "exploring" as we called it,
carrying on with that busy,
whorish Janey after
ten years of marriage and six kids.

He'd make two or three day trips
to that woman
while I worked two jobs,
one at the community hospital,
the other cleaning offices at night.
I expected a lifetime of romance,
I didn't figure on ten years!
And to make it worse,

when I spoke back to my mama
and papa by the bed that night,
Otis overheard me
and, not seeing anyone there himself,
thought I was talking in my sleep
to some other man,
and he was always saying
how he'd wish he'd find one thing
I did wrong so he wouldn't
feel so bad about the way
he treated me.

He started cussing and carrying on
and my folks just
sort of went their way,
but I'd taken their message to heart
and the next day I left
with all the children, and
a couple days later
Otis showed up at my brother's
where I was staying
showing up with an iron pipe and
a lotta anger, saying
he was gonna whip me on home.
I thought how hard I worked
for that man, killing myself
everyday, and I looked at him
and said, "God, give me the strength
to whip this man's behind..."

And I took that pipe
out of his hands
and but for God's graces
I would've killed him.
It was a hot ending to a hot marriage,
and I'll always thank my
mama and papa for dropping by
the bedside that night,

showing me a way out.
Yes, I expected a lifetime of romance;
I didn't figure on ten years.

Last Wave

ROSIE MITCHELL'S "LAST WAVE" is, simply, a story about the last time she saw her brother alive. She recalled a few moments from his life, and without an onslaught of biographical matter it was easy to see what was at the heart of her recollection—the deep love for a brother and a genuine belief that she would see him again in another life. The wave that didn't occur is the wave, of course, she keeps with her through the years, knowing it will appear "big and beautiful" when she sees him again. ∎

Last Wave
Rosie Mitchell

HE WAS WEARING A red shirt. He always looked good in bright colors, because they seemed to reflect his spirit.

He was a fussy dresser too. Never a wrinkle in his shirt, even if he had nowhere to go. Lately, he didn't go too many places. But as a foster grandfather he still took pride in his appearance, and dressed handsomely while he met with the young children there in Newburg, NY.

As a young man, J.C. worked hard. He had to quit school down on our farm in Tuskegee, Alabama. He was only fourteen, and though he loved to read and write, there was no money and a lot of work.

And he worked hard, but with love, as a cook in the Army during the war years of the forties. And later, he cooked at the veterans hospital as well. In Newburg that day nine years ago, that warm spring day with the sun glowing down on us, and the buds bursting on the trees, and a few tulips showing themselves in the corner of his backyard, he cooked then too. I remember the aroma of cornbread and chicken filling the kitchen that day as J.C. cooked and laughed and his daughter Yvonne and my daughter Yvette and J.C.'s grandchildren Charles and Stacey sat around the table. He made the most delicious dressing I've ever had, and those peas were as black-eyed and tender as J.C. himself.

It did seem kind of strange, thinking back, how he gave me that money that day and said, "This'll help you on your way, Sis," and then he handed me his favorite tea cup as well....

On the bus that afternoon, all of us waved at J.C. through the window as he saw us off there on the sidewalk. For some reason though, he wouldn't wave back. He just turned around and began walking away as the bus moved forward like a great old ship.

Now I know my brother couldn't bear to wave goodbye—because he died that night, just a few hours later, alone in Newburg. The pain in his heart as it gave out that day made its way to my heart, where I hold it with his memory. I still sit in my living room expecting a phone call from him, and when I collect the mail, sometimes I expect one of his letters.

I'm sure he's up there cooking for someone, someone tasting that dressing and shaking his head so. And I know he saved that last wave for one big beautiful wave when I see him again.

Upstate

THERE HAS BEEN FOR many years a large migrant population near Rochester, and the apple orchards and fertile croplands have attracted a lot of Southerners to upstate New York, and of course many ended up settling in the area. Alberta William gives us a vivid glimpse of life in a migrant camp, recalling a particular season in Savannah after moving up from Florida in a "tranp" truck—a term I didn't get right (I thought she was saying *tramp*) until the third revision of the poem. The image of her two suitors sitting in Alberta's shed, eyeing each other all night, will stay with me forever— especially when she leaves them there to watch her little boy while she goes out dancing! I also liked her tone of resignation—"might as well marry one of these crazy guys." Alberta's expression, "traveling free," strikes a universal chord—the independent spirit that exists in the midst of a life of long hours of hard work, transience, and poverty. ■

Upstate
Alberta William

I CAUGHT THE TRANP truck
going north
leaving Florida behind, my three-year-old son
at my side.
It was June, and the celery was ripe
in upstate New York, and the sunshine
baked the necks of us migrants
as we bumped along the roads of Georgia,
the Carolinas, Virginia, and up.

I wanted to see the world,
being twenty-one and needing to be free.
And when the driver said Savannah New York,
well, it sounded like Georgia
under a big, northern, money sky,
and I found a seat in the back
of that tranp truck, twenty or more of us,
sleeping along the road at night
under the trees, on the sweet beds
of grass in this big
endless country, traveling free, traveling free....

I picked crops all day
and cuddled with little Thomas in
our shed at night, the two-burner oil stove
warm as our hearts.
And I wasn't there a week
when Albert William and Johnny Scott
showed up, boys who worked
on my daddy's farm down in Florida.
They were working
at the Stoney-Lonesome Camp near by,
and had heard I was there.
And from that first night they wouldn't
let me alone.

They'd sit all night in my shed,
on the only two chairs I had,
each waiting for the other to leave,
so stubborn and both sweet on me.
Sometimes I'd go out
the back door, leave them watching Thomas,
sitting there with their eyes
on each other,
and I'd go out to the juke joint
and snap my fingers
and dance, traveling free, dancing so free...

On the eighth week, last week
of picking,
I said to myself as they both sat there,
might as well marry one of
these crazy guys.
And sure enough, before
the tranp truck pulled up,
Albert William came by in a '36 Ford
and said, I'll drive you back...
the wind blowing, the countryside
moving past, and me seeing that red Southern
sun
and thinking it's hanging like a lamp
somewhere down in that Florida sky....

But we stopped in Ashboro, North Carolina—
for three months that is!
At Albert's parents' place.
He told them we were *married*,
and all I could do was shrug my shoulders
and say to myself, "If that's what he say..."

And a few months later, back on
my dad's farm among the greens and beets
and radishes, and with even Johnny Scott,
back home and picking oranges

and drinking too much rum,
I thought again I might as well marry
this crazy guy,
and when Albert asked my daddy,
that's exactly what I did.

It's hard to recall the years,
but when I think back
to where I've been and what I've done,
I often feel the bumps of the benches
in the back of the tranp truck,
and the songs we sang on our way
to somewhere new, sleeping under the trees
and picking the early fruit
in a field no one cared much about....
I close my eyes,
no place and everywhere ahead,
just traveling free, nothing to lose,
the road upstate and we're traveling free.

After Mama's Death

BACK IN THE TWENTIES and thirties, it was not
uncommon for young girls (and boys) to be thrust
into the role of "homemaker" at the death of a par-
ent. There were, in fact, special classes for girls as
young as eleven and twelve which taught them
basic home skills—cooking, cleaning, and child-
rearing. Sometimes they were called "dunce class-
es," but the sad fact is they were necessary in times
when families were large, poor, and sometimes
missing a parent. Louise NiCastro describes such a
time in her life, when she took over her deceased
mother's responsibilities. What makes it especially
interesting to me is the way we are introduced to
several layers of emotions—not just the initial
impact of the mother's death and the concern for
the infant twins, but the story of her sister sudden-
ly separated from her school life, and the father,
lost, out of work, counting on his young daughters
to keep the household together. And all of this
encompassed by the wonderful "kid's tale" of the
ghost on the wall and the thoughts of her mother
who might be watching over her. When the young
Louise looks in on the family members as they
sleep, we see the poignant fusion of innocent girl
and burdened woman, of exuberance and exhaus-
tion, of fear and strength. ■

After Mama's Death

Louise NiCastro

THE VOICE WAS ABRUPT, clear:
"If you don't pick up
your twins by Monday, we'll put them
up for adoption...."

It was right after the funeral.
The doctor was trying to revive
my sister, who had passed out
just as my mother was being lowered
into the ground.
My sister's light brown hair was long
and beautiful. She looked like
a Madonna stretched out on the
white bedspread. She was
lovely and vulnerable, and for the moment
stiff as a board.

There were eight of us,
and with me being the oldest at twenty,
it was up to me to take care of
the house, especially
the infants, born a few days
before my mother died.
I had to work too,
pulling bastings at Hickey-Freeman clothes,
because my father not only
lost his wife, he'd lost his job too.

My sister, so beautiful
and out cold, would have to quit school,
and perhaps she knew that
in her unconsciousness.

We spent our last money that night
on a taxi ride

to pick up Yolanda and Mafalda,
the newborn twins at the hospital.
Once they were home
it seemed there was no time
to think about anything.
My sister recovered one moment,
and learned to change diapers the next.
As soon as I got home
from the factory, I began washing clothes,
sewing and cooking.
Sometimes I'd finish up
by mopping the floor at midnight,
when everyone was asleep....

And it was about a month later,
one clear October night,
when I hung the mop on the clothesline
in the backyard to dry, the stars
scattered across the sky.
Just as I began to warm the babies' bottles
for their midnight feeding,
I heard the wind begin to howl,
and outside the kitchen window
the moonlight beamed like a spotlight.
When I looked out
I gasped, and took a deep,
fearful breath.
On the wall of the house next door
appeared a silhouette of a woman.
She was wearing a cape
and her hair was blowing wildly in the wind.

I closed my eyes,
but the ghosts of the season
flew across my mind, and with them
the image of my mother.
I looked once more,
and the dark woman swung back and forth

in the bright moonlight
that lit the side of our neighbor's house.
Maybe, I thought,
we weren't as good to the babies
as we should have been,
or perhaps the house wasn't kept
as clean as my mother would have wanted.

I was afraid to look out
any more, feeling I'd die if I did.
The wind sounded like the chorus of death.
I was so scared,
I couldn't even look in the mirror
to check on myself....
Then I heard the wind gather itself
for another trumpeting blow
against the night,
and in my mind I saw the ghost
my mother spoke of in the stories she
told us on Hallowe'en.
In the backyard I saw
a gust of wind flip the mop off the clothesline,
and then, on the moonlit wall
of the house next door
the woman was gone, simply vanished.
The wind seemed to die a little
there in my heart,
and then I understood it was
the shadow of the mop on the wall,
and all the ghosts and demons
were in my mind.
I woke up the babies
and fed the sleeping beauties.
I looked in on the loveliness of my sister,
dreaming perhaps of the frolic
of school days she was missing.
I looked in on the hard,
troublesome sleep of my father, so lost

in the waking world.
I set out the breakfast table
before I went to sleep,
and in my moonlit thoughts
as I touched my head to the pillow
I saw my mother,
not as the dark silhouette of the mop,
but beautiful, serene,
touching my brow with her warm hand,
whispering her love for all of us
she left behind, her words
rising and falling,
like the wind outside,
like the heart's gentle swell in my chest.

Giving Up the Cakes

I ASKED THE GROUP of elderly black women in my program to remember what the holidays were like, especially Thanksgiving, since it's always been a favorite holiday of mine, and since too I imagined there was very little to be thankful for in those poor times. How naive I am! And that's why I'm always the student in our oral history group encounters. Sarah McClellan describes beautifully the simple joys of her early Thanksgivings. It's a reminder for us, of course, to be thankful for what we have, and it's fitting that Sarah remembered some verse from a prayer she used to recite as a child; that the Lord's Truth "endures through all generations."■

Giving Up the Cakes
Sarah McClellan

THEM OLD MARKET BASKETS were heavy,
swinging so awkward-like between
me and my brother Edgar,
that big old plain cake sitting there in it,
looking so good, and me and Edgar
wishing we could just sit down
and eat that cake up all by ourselves,
and leave that big basket
under the bridge till we made our way back home
from school later on.

It was Thanksgiving,
so we had no books to carry, no lessons
to recite that day, just a picnic
in the schoolyard.
And when me and my brother
saw all those cakes lined up on the table
—jelly cakes, pineapple,
cocoa block cakes and white caramel cakes,
we was glad we brought ours to share,
and it was in the midst of plenty
we all felt so charitable toward each other,
passing out all those slices of cake
and eating till we couldn't eat no more.

I was eleven then,
and I can see that teacher clapping her hands
and running with her skirt hitched up,
hop-scotching and hide-and-seeking with us kids.
I can see Edgar laughing in the sunlight,
his teeth so white, and his knee-blouses
already stained with grass.
It was the year, I remember,
that we sent up the peace flag in the schoolyard;
the end of the big War,

and you could hear the people screaming
and hollering from the rooftops and cotton
fields,
and all of us danced in a circle
in the schoolyard, holding hands and
thanking the Lord for the peace of our souls....

On Thanksgiving, each student
had to recite some verse with thanks in it
somewhere, and I remember mine:

> Give thanks unto the Lord,
> His Mercy is good.
> His Truth endures through all generations.

On our way home, Edgar and me
swang that basket between us,
and we could feel the cool winter air
sweeping through the trees.
We didn't raise no turkeys then,
but when we got home
my ma had waiting for us
greens and cornbread, chicken
and plenty of milk and butter, and
molasses for her buttermilk biscuits.
But we were filled with cakes.
We were happy with those cakes.

My Certificate in Negro History

THIS IS A STORY THAT has to be told—not just initially by Sarah McClellan whose story it is, but by others who want to know what it was like in mid-century America in the South for those who hungered not just for food and shelter, but for their own sense of history, the hidden source of their identity. It must be difficult for our young people to imagine a grown woman, tired all day from picking crops, taking care of her grandkids, making her way to clandestine meetings at night, trying to learn, as Sarah puts it, "What ought to have been hers all along." There was real danger down in Mississippi, the freedom fighter's life literally on the line, as she hid in different houses between the lessons she gave to these poor but ambitious blacks. When Sarah's story was published in the Gannett newspaper in Rochester, she was given a special certificate from the New York state legislature. "There'll come another day," says Sarah, "when all that silence will make you sing." Hers are not only words of wisdom, they are at the heart of oral histories, and that particular statement could be an epigraph for this entire collection. ■

My Certificate in Negro History
Sarah McClellan

"YOU SHOULD HAVE BEEN there to see
such a raggedy, hungry bunch,
1400 of us waiting in the rain and mud
for a bag of yellow meal, lard
and eggs, lines so long
we'd have to camp out, or go back
two or three days..."

It was the freedom fighter, Pat,
a sweet girl from Chicago,
who asked me to write that letter
to President Johnson
when we was hungry and tired
down in Cleveland, Mississippi in '66.
We'd meet at the closed-down
Methodist school for a three-day meeting
and Pat would give us
some Negro history schooling, something
which should have been ours
all along. And in the evening too,
in our little town, after picking
cotton all day, I'd take my
grandchildren, Curtis E. and Linda Pearl,
and we'd meet under the good light
of the moon, and in the deeper light
of our eyes,
there in the churchyard where Pat
would show us photos and read to us
about Negro sisters and brothers
like Harriet Tubman, who done
carried babies on her own back
and drove stubborn women through the hills
at night and into freedom tunnels
of the underground railroad....

My letter appeared in the evening news,
and with it
a hundred signatures from those
who struggled to write out the proud letters
of their names.
Times were a getting tense, oh Lord;
you could feel it in the voice
of the postmaster's wife
when I went down to mail a letter
and she'd ask if I knew
where the girl from Chicago, the freedom
fighter was a-staying:
The storekeeper would ask too,
and so did the owner of the dry goods store.
It seemed the more we knew
the quieter we were forced to become.

So we hid Pat from night to night in a
different place—staying awhile
with the minister's wife, but even that
wasn't safe.
Just down the road in Mississippi
we were told of the brush-hopper deaths,
one little colored boy
and two freedom fighters found dead
(and decomposed
under a brush hopper)
in the sprawling well-cared yard of a
lady aristocrat who swore
they were the remains of an old horse.
And in Honanah
there was going to be a march,
and my son, Sammy Lewis, said Mama, don't
go—and by the look in his eye
I thought I'm old enough to mind my children,
and sure enough,
that's where Meredith was shot.

And one day, someone said, Sarah.
the President sent us
a plane full of food—he got your letter.
So we made our way
to the old schoolhouse, and we
watched the county prisoners carry it in
in their grey-and-white stripes, big as
my three fingers.
Someone said the canned meat was
ground-up cow hearts, but we didn't care,
we were hungry.
We waited in line
for the coffee and yellow meal and grits.
Some judge stood on the steps for awhile
and stared us down;
then he sent a young white man
down among us to take photographs of us.
And someone else asked
where Pat, the Yankee freedom fighter was
at....

It was just the night before, in fact,
that Pat handed me
my certificate in Negro History,
saying what a fine student I had been.
"I don't want to go," she said,
"but my time is up," and then she gave
me a hug.
Holding that certificate in my hand and I knew
that a person is a person,
and out of one blood
God created all nations....

On our way home, my grandchildren
and me struggled with our food cartons.
The postmaster's wife stopped us
and she asked,

"Sarah, by the way, you know where
that white girl is...."

I told my grandchildren then, like
I'm telling you'all now.
One of these days you'll run into something
that you'll be quiet about.

And there'll be another day
when all that silence will make you sing.

Ross Talarico

Ross Talarico's poetry has appeared in more than 200 publica
tions, including *The Atlantic, The Nation, The American Poetr*
Review and *The Iowa Review*. He is writer-in-residence for th
city of Rochester, New York—a position unique in America—
where he directs a community-based program, working with
people of all ages, backgrounds and interests. Mr Talarico wa
awarded the prestigious Lillian Fairchild Award from th
University of Rochester for his book of vignettes and poetry, *A*
Things As They Are: Recollections of the Sixties and Beyond.

Hilary Masters

Hilary Masters' most recent selection of stories is *Success*, (St
Martins Press). Mr Masters now lives in Pittsburgh, where h
directs the creative writing program at Carnegie-Mellor
University.